Living Our
Beliefs

The United Methodist Way

Second Edition

Kenneth L. Carder

DISCIPLESHIP
RESOURCES

Cover design by Shawn Lancaster
Interior design by PerfecType, Nashville, TN

ISBN 978-0-88177-571-6

Library of Congress Control Number: 2009933654

Printed in the United States of America

DR571

CONTENTS

FOREWORD

I t is my pleasure to introduce this second edition of Kenneth Carder's *Living Our Beliefs: The United Methodist Way*. I still remember my sense over a decade ago, on reading the first edition, that it was a major expression of United Methodists reclaiming the balance of John Wesley's wisdom about cultivating Christian life and witness. While we had kept alive Wesley's emphasis on experiencing the forgiving love of God, and we emulated (indeed, over-emulated) his penchant for organization, a variety of factors had led us to downplay the vital role that Wesley assigned to instruction in Christian beliefs and participation in spiritual disciplines.

Wesley's mature wisdom in this regard is evident in one of his last sermons, titled "Causes of the Inefficacy of Christianity."[1] The sermon opens with Wesley's assessment that the reason Christian communities around the globe have done so little good in the world is that they are producing so few real Christians. He then identified two key factors of typical church life that contribute to this lamentable state: 1) few churches expect or assist members to attain adequate understanding of Christian beliefs; and 2) of those churches which attend to Christian teaching, many lack corresponding emphasis on Christian disciplines—including the specific discipline of self-denial.

Every journey is oriented by its goal. For the early Methodists, the goal was to become faithful and mature disciples of Christ. This meant far more than only affirming Christ as their Lord or having an assurance of his pardoning love. They longed for what they saw promised in scripture—the transformation of their sin-distorted attitudes and dispositions into ever-greater conformity with Christ's abiding love for God, for neighbor, and for the whole creation. In other words, while early Methodists celebrated the freedom from sin that comes in the new birth, they fervently desired that greater freedom for walking in God's life-giving ways and participating in God's saving mission.

Much of Wesley's leadership of the Methodist movement was devoted to challenging inadequate and distorted conceptions of Christian teaching that he discerned were contributing to the inadequate (and sometimes perverse) lives of many Christians. He was equally concerned to articulate positively—for believer and skeptic alike—the central Christian convictions about the nature of God, the nature of humanity, the nature of sin and evil, and the scope of God's salvific mission. Wesley emphasized the role of pastors as theologians and teachers in interchanges with his fellow Anglican priests, and he embodied that role in his own pastoral work.

The prominence of Wesley's concern for doctrine has been obscured for some by his sharp criticism of equating "being Christian" with mere affirmation of correct doctrine. But this was not a dismissal of doctrine. It was an insistence that Christian teaching is intended to shape the core convictions and dispositions that guide our choices and actions in the world. Wesley imbibed this conviction about the formative intent of doctrine from the Early Church. Their precedent also led him to appreciate the most effective means of helping to instill abiding Christian convictions and dispositions. Sporadic exhortations are not sufficient. Recurrent practices most deeply shape us. So Wesley made regular participation in worship, scripture study, prayer, and the like central to the Methodist way of life—as specified in the *General Rules.* Through this participation, early Methodists immersed themselves in the whole of the Christian story and allowed it to form (and reform) the breadth of their convictions and dispositions.

If recognition of the vital role of practices in appropriation of the transforming work of the Holy Spirit was central to the early Methodist way, Wesley's appreciation for the full range of these practices was its deep wisdom. He often summarized this appreciation in a saying from the early church: "The soul and the body make a [human], the Spirit and discipline make a Christian." This proverb reminds us that humans are holistic creatures and that our actions rarely flow from intellectual motivations alone. As such, renewal of our sin-distorted convictions and dispositions is most effectively nurtured within a set of disciplines that address all the dimensions of our nature.

Nothing drew more of Wesley's attention in shepherding the early Methodist movement than weaving together such a rich set of means of grace as the core of their way of life. Alongside standard practices of corporate worship, he commended innovative practices such as the Love Feast and Covenant Service. While prescribing personal devotional reading and regular immersion in scripture, he stressed the need for concurrent participation in corporate settings ("no holiness but social holiness"). Ever conscious of the value of practices that increase rational understanding of Christian truth, he put special emphasis on complementary practices where the empowering presence of the Spirit is mediated through touch, taste, and tears. He gave particular prominence to the formative power of the faith sung, of small groups that provide support and accountability, and of regular participation in works of mercy. Finally, he recognized the crucial role of mentors, of those who are far enough along in their journey with Christ to be able to say with Paul, "Be imitators of me, as I am of Christ" (1 Corinthians 11:1).

Through his long and fruitful ministry, Bishop Carder has come to share Wesley's appreciation for the importance of attending to Christian belief and practice—and to the vital connection between these two. He has also inherited Wesley's ability to speak in "plain words for plain people," combining accessibility with deep insight and affective engagement. When Wesley was asked where to turn for a reliable introduction to Anglican teaching, he consistently recommended Bishop John Pearson's *Exposition on the Creed*. When I am asked where

to turn for a reliable introduction to United Methodist teaching, I am
delighted that I can point in the same way to a bishop of our church.
If there is a difference, it is that Bishop Carder does not just exposit
United Methodist belief; true to the spirit of Wesley, he invites us to
live our beliefs.

Randy L. Maddox
William Kellon Quick Professor of Wesleyan and Methodist Studies
Duke Divinity School

INTRODUCTION

A long-existing notion is that United Methodists are indifferent to doctrine. As one person said to me, "You can believe anything and be a Methodist, just so you are sincere." Such a misperception has deep historical and cultural roots and it contributes to the absence of sound doctrine and theology in many contemporary United Methodist classrooms and pulpits.

Methodism began as a renewal movement within the Church of England and did not originate in doctrinal debates and controversies. The basic faith tenets of the Anglican Church were accepted and often presumed by the early Methodists. Though there were and are distinctive emphases, the core doctrines of the Methodist family are held in common with the broader Christian community.

As a renewal movement in the eighteenth century, the focus was less on defining and defending distinctive doctrines and beliefs and more on experiences and practices that embodied the doctrines and beliefs. On the American frontier with its individualism and revivalism, more emphasis began to be placed on "right experience" than right beliefs. The original meaning of *Methodist* as those who with discipline and accountability grow in grace took on an institutional and organizational reference. Methodists became known for their structures and polity more than their beliefs.

American democracy also contributed to diminished interest in doctrine. In the word of historian Nathan Hatch, religion was "democratized."[1] The denominational landscape offered multiple doctrinal and ecclesial options. The exercise of individual autonomy took precedence over communal conformity to creeds, and sincerity and tolerance became primary marks of religious faithfulness.

We have experienced in recent years a renewed interest in discovering our cultural and religious roots, and an explosion of scholarship in various religious traditions is taking place. The Methodist tradition is no exception as an increasing number of Wesley and Methodist scholars reflect on the events, theology, and practices of the tradition and the implications for the contemporary world.

The scholars are affirming that doctrine and beliefs are critical components of Methodist identity. But Christian doctrine serves two important functions in the United Methodist tradition. Doctrine and creedal formulations serve as the lens through which we view the world. They provide the framework by which we interpret and live our lives.

Furthermore, beliefs function in the service of character formation, faith development, missional engagement, and evangelization. Wesley's emphasis on practical divinity prevented doctrines and beliefs from becoming primarily theoretical speculations, academic pursuits, or legal evidence against heretics. Wesley's preoccupation with the way to salvation caused him to evaluate doctrines in terms of their impact on living. His principal concern was the relationship between beliefs and behavior, doctrine and discipleship, theological concepts and Christian character.

In other words, beliefs are to be lived; doctrine is to be practiced. The authenticity of beliefs lies in their ability to shape people and communities into the image of Christ and to promote holiness and happiness. Do they promote love for God and neighbor? The important test of the validity of doctrines and beliefs for United Methodists is the kind of character they produce in individuals and communities and the actions they inspire in the world. That is the United Methodist way.

Utilizing Wesley's sermons, the approved doctrinal/theological statement in *The United Methodist Book of Discipline*, the liturgical resources in *The United Methodist Hymnal*, and other materials, this book attempts to identify and clarify United Methodist beliefs and their relevance for living as disciples of Jesus Christ. Laity and clergy are encouraged to use the book as a resource for living their beliefs, which is the United Methodist way.

The book originated in response to an invitation from the staff of Discipleship Resources at the General Board of Discipleship, who recognized a need for a resource to be used by laity and clergy in identifying and living United Methodist beliefs. Being asked to write and revise such a resource is a distinct honor, and with honor always comes responsibility. George Donigian and Doug Hagler and the staff have provided invaluable support in enabling me to fulfill the responsibility.

I am indebted to many scholars and friends who have deepened and broadened my understanding of Wesleyan theology and tradition. Among them are my colleagues at Duke Divinity School—Stephen Gunter, Richard Heitzenrater, Greg Jones, Randy Maddox, and Laceye Warner. Long-time friends Theodore Jennings, James C. Logan, M. Douglas Meeks, Bobby McClain, and David Lowes Watson have been mentors and colleagues for more than thirty years and continue to inspire and teach me. I am also grateful to numerous laity and clergy colleagues whose lives and ministry embody the Methodist way.

Toward the end of his long years of living and proclaiming his beliefs, John Wesley reflected upon the future of the Methodist move ment. By all statistical measurements, the movement was strong and continuing to grow throughout Europe and America. Yet, the apparent weakening of Methodist moral influence, evangelical commitment, and missional involvement disturbed Wesley. He wrote in 1786:

> I am not afraid that the people called Methodists should ever cease to exist either in Europe or America. But I am afraid lest they should only exist as a dead sect, having the form of religion without the power. And this undoubtedly will be the case unless they hold fast both the doctrine, spirit, and discipline with which they first set out.[2]

Prospects for renewal are enhanced if contemporary Methodists live the doctrine, discipline, and spirit with which the movement began. That is the United Methodist way!

1

Why a United Methodist?

Richard Allen, the founder of the African Methodist Episcopal Church, was born into slavery on February 14, 1760. At the age of seventeen, he was converted by the preaching of Freeborn Garrettson and joined the Methodist Society. He was licensed to preach in 1782. One of two black preachers at the organizing conference of the Methodist Episcopal Church in 1784, he became a member of the Old St. George's Methodist Society in Philadelphia. While praying at St. George's in 1794, he and a few black colleagues were literally pulled from their knees by an official of the Society. Allen and his friends left St. George's and subsequently formed the AME Church.

Although some white Methodists cruelly mistreated him, Richard Allen wrote, "I feel thankful that ever I heard a Methodist preach. We are beholden to the Methodists, under God, for the light of the Gospel we enjoy."[1] He was asked to be the pastor of a non-Methodist African Church in Philadelphia. He offered the following as his reason for refusing the position: "I told them I could not accept their offer, as I was a Methodist . . . I informed them that I could not be anything else but a Methodist . . ."[2]

Waning Denominational Loyalty

Few United Methodists today consider that they "could not be anything else but a Methodist." Church loyalty is related less to denominational labels and historic roots than programs offered, convenience of location, and family and friendship ties. Denominationalism, as has been known and practiced in the United States during the last two hundred years, may be coming to an end. It is not uncommon for persons to be members of several different denominations in their lifetimes. The differences among denominations seem less significant than the differences among congregations within the same denomination.

Denominational identity no longer has the appeal it once enjoyed. Preachers could, a few decades ago, attract a following through denominational chauvinism. Condemning other churches and extolling the superiority of one's own denomination could build churches. Such a message today receives but isolated positive response. Most preachers now are far more critical of their own denomination than other communions.

Some local congregations have chosen to de-emphasize their denominational identity or sever the ties altogether. Several United Methodist churches downplay their relationship with the denomination by removing "United Methodist" from the signage and replacing it with more generic names such as "Community Church," "Church of the Covenant," "Fellowship Chapel," or other labels designed to attract those to whom denominational identity may be perceived as a barrier.

Sociologists point to many factors in the apparent erosion of denominational loyalty, including a transient population less anchored to one city or job. As people move to new communities and shop for places to live, they also shop for places to worship. Additionally, the rise of individualized faith that borrows from many traditions contributes to waning denominational allegiance. Religious pluralism and the rise of spirituality without institutional identity erode faithfulness to a particular denomination or tradition. An increasing number of people claim to be spiritual but shun affiliation with institutional religion.

Another factor contributing to suspicion of denominations are the dysfunction and controversies that have characterized many of the mainline churches in America. Americans like to associate with success and growth. The loss of cultural prominence and statistical decline among the mainline denominations spawns suspicion and undermines support. Conflicts over sexuality, Bible interpretation, and denominational pronouncements on volatile issues exacerbate cynicism toward organized religion in general and denominations in particular.

Diminished denominational appeal, however, is not the total picture. Since Alex Haley's *Roots: The Saga of an American Family*, published in 1976 and subsequently made into a television miniseries, there has been a renewed interest in discovering our heritage. History matters! Identities are formed by the practices, experiences, and beliefs of the past. Individuals, institutions, and cultures have roots and those roots influence the present and help shape the future.

Many denominations are attempting to rediscover their identity and heritage as one means of defining their mission for the future. As the prophet admonished a people who found themselves in a new cultural context, "Look to the rock from which you were hewn, and to the quarry from which you were dug" (Isaiah 51:1). One might argue that a reason for the decline among the denominations is amnesia, the loss of memory. Lost memory means lost identity and those with amnesia have to depend upon others to define them. A church with no memory gets its identity from the culture and loses its power to influence the culture.

Are the trends toward less denominational loyalty and renewed interest in theological or doctrinal identity contradictory and mutually exclusive? If denominational loyalty is waning, why bother with learning the historic doctrines and beliefs of particular traditions? Why be concerned about what Methodists believe? Why not simply talk about what Christians believe and ignore the distinctiveness of denominations? After all, is not what we share in common far more significant than our differences? Or, is the recovery of doctrinal and theological roots and distinctiveness a potential means to renewed vitality and mission?

Nourished by Common Roots

These important questions merit response. First, our primary loyalty must be to Jesus Christ and the Christian gospel. We are Christians first! Reception into membership of a United Methodist Church is first and foremost membership in the church universal. Baptized members of other denominations are received into membership in The United Methodist Church without being re-baptized. Professions of faith made in other denominational contexts are considered valid. Since United Methodism is not a "confessional" church with one creed to which members are asked to subscribe, membership preparation tends to give less emphasis to distinctive United Methodist doctrinal positions and more focus on what Christians hold in common.

The doctrinal/theological statement in *The Book of Discipline*[3] identifies the following as basic Christian affirmations that we share in common with other communions:

- We confess belief in the triune God—Father, Son, and Holy Spirit.
- We hold a faith in the mystery of salvation in and through Jesus Christ.
- God's redemptive love is realized in human life by the activity of the Holy Spirit, both in personal experience and in the community of believers.
- We are part of Christ's universal church when by adoration, proclamation, and service we become conformed to Christ.
- The reign of God is both a present and future reality.
- Scripture is authoritative in matters of faith.
- Our justification as sinners is by grace through faith.
- The church is in need of continual reformation and renewal.
- The essential oneness of the church in Jesus Christ is affirmed in the historic creeds.

Methodism's doctrinal and theological foundation, therefore, has more to do with emphases than with distinctiveness. Certain emphases within the church universal have formed Methodism's theological identity. *The Book of Discipline* states: "Nourished by common roots of this shared Christian heritage, the branches of Christ's Church have developed diverse traditions that enlarge our store of shared understandings. Our avowed ecumenical commitment as United Methodists is to gather our own doctrinal emphases into the larger Christian unity, there to be made more meaningful in a richer whole."[4]

Just as we all share in a common humanity but are enriched by distinctive heritages and traits, Christians share in common primary commitment to Jesus Christ and are made richer by particular faith stories and emphases. Our officially approved position affirms: "If we are to offer our best gifts to the common Christian treasury, we must make a deliberate effort as a church to strive for critical self understanding. It is as Christians involved in ecumenical partnership that we embrace and examine our distinctive heritage."[5]

A Movement of Mission and Reform

Methodism began as a mission and reform movement within the Church of England. Methodism did not arise in response to doctrinal controversy. The leaders did not set out to reformulate doctrine but to summon people to experience and live the grace of God and to grow in their knowledge and love of God. John Wesley said that God had raised up the Methodists to "reform the nation, particularly the Church, and to spread scriptural holiness over the land."[6]

Reform and mission grew out of the early Methodists' experience and understanding of the Triune God and God's presence at work in the world. Doctrinal interpretation, evangelical proclamation, discipleship formation, and social witness were inseparable components of a vital relationship with God. The results helped to spawn a spiritual and moral revival in England and America.

The conditions existing in England in the 1700s are parallel to those confronting us in the twenty-first century. The Enlightenment and the emerging scientific revolution offered alternative views of the world and new means of dealing with personal and societal problems. The industrial revolution intensified the economic disparity between the rich and the poor and brought a new wave of exploitation. The poor were depersonalized. Children were at risk as they labored in the factories and mines. Slavery was a thriving business and existed with minimal protest from the established religious institutions. Suffering and death stalked the human family. Medical care was beyond the reach of the masses. Hedonism increased as the strict morality of Victorian England gave way to moral relativity, freedom, and uncertainty. The established church lost its appeal to the masses, particularly the poor. Its moral and ethical influence was minimal. Crime and violence threatened society. Prisons and the gallows were prevalent methods of dealing with the rising crime rate. The nation seemed to have lost its spiritual and moral compass and moorings.

In Need of Revival

Few people within the church question that the contemporary world stands in need of spiritual and moral revival. We are confronted with the inadequacy of old answers to familiar questions and uncertain answers to new questions. Our society has become increasingly secularized; religion has been compartmentalized and marginalized in the public consciousness and institutions. Exalting the scientific method as the supreme path to truth has rendered divine revelation suspect. The promotion of individual freedom, self-expression, and self-fulfillment above community responsibility and social responsibility has undermined civic accountability and love of neighbor. Morality and ethics have been relativized and left to personal preferences and expediency, resulting in moral uncertainty at best and moral anarchy at worst.

The disparity between the rich and the poor grows wider, and millions of people are dying from a lack of life's basic necessities. Violence and crime stalk our neighborhoods. Longer prison sentences and the death penalty have again become the primary solutions offered for the problems of crime and violence. War continues as the costliest and persistent means of settling disputes among nations. Mainline churches are declining in membership and influence. They seldom include the impoverished masses in their membership; and the voice of the church on the great issues of our time has been muffled or relegated to narrow political agendas.

In spite of phenomenal scientific and technological advances and economic growth, unparalleled suffering plagues the human family. While many diseases—which once meant certain death—have been removed, new diseases such as HIV/AIDS now threaten entire populations. Science and technology have increased the speed and expanse of transportation and communication; they have also created weapons that killed more people in the twentieth century than in all previous centuries combined. Biology and chemistry extended the life span of millions but they have also created potential for devastating drug addiction and its accompanying suffering.

Economic wealth has greatly increased and new medical breakthroughs are occurring daily, and yet more people are dying of poverty-related causes than ever in history. Even though most nations denounce the exploitation of children, approximately ten to twenty million children die each year from poverty. Although human rights came to the forefront of concern in the twentieth century, we continue to persecute and slaughter millions of people because of race, gender, religion, and national origin. The whole planet is now in peril from global warming, environmental degradation, the depletion of indispensable resources, contamination of the food supply, and the threat of catastrophic nuclear war.

Ours is an age of both unparalleled progress and incomparable agony. The suffering is extensive, the dangers are of cataclysmic proportions, and the problems are monumentally complex. But the possibilities for resolution are unmatched and immeasurable. For the first time in human history, the scientific, technological, and economic resources are available to prevent many premature deaths, to enhance the quality of life of all people, and to forge a new future of justice and peace. What is lacking are the moral vision and political will. Such vision and will are at the heart of the Church's mission! Without a spiritual and moral revival, the future of the earth is in jeopardy and the suffering is likely to intensify and encompass even more of the human family.

Plain Doctrine . . . Good Discipline

A recovery of the theological emphases, which sparked the Wesleyan revival in the eighteenth century, has the potential of igniting a revival in the twenty-first century. Spiritual renewal comes as a gift from God. It does not result from new programs or structures offered by the church. Efforts to revitalize the church through strategic planning processes, restructuring institutions, and programmatic emphases have a role to play, but without a firm grounding in the Triune God, they are destined to fail. Only by sharing in God's life and mission through the power of the Holy Spirit does renewal take place. Without that vital sharing in the presence, purposes, and action of God, all strategies and structures are but pious idols and improved means to unimproved ends. The traditional Methodist summons to "experience the justifying and sanctifying grace of God and encourage people to grow in the knowledge and love of God through the personal and corporate disciplines of the Christian life"[7] remains our primary challenge.

Richard Allen's reason for being a Methodist had nothing to do with denominational superiority or doctrinal uniqueness. He attributed the Methodists' effectiveness in awakening and converting people to the gospel to "plain doctrine and . . . good discipline."[8] His concern far exceeded institutional chauvinism or even church growth. Allen was convinced that Methodism offered a doorway into the life of God and a means of sharing in Christ's ministry to the world.

Efforts to clarify the beliefs of United Methodists are not directed toward creating denominational pride or setting The United Methodist Church apart from other churches. The goal is to use the Wesleyan tradition as a doorway into knowledge and love of God. As a branch is nourished through its roots, Methodism's doctrinal and theological roots are means by which God can nourish us with divine grace and graft us into Christ's mission in the world.

God's preoccupation is the transformation of the world, not the statistical growth of the institutional church. The church is an instrument of God's mission and God calls it to be a sign, foretaste, and vehicle of God's new heaven and new earth. Its identity is in its relationship with God and its involvement in Christ's ministry of reconciliation in a broken, suffering, and sinful world. It must therefore ask anew the basic questions: Who is the God known in Jesus Christ? Where is God present and what is God doing in the world? What is the appropriate response to the nature, presence, and action of God? These are among the questions that are addressed in our Wesleyan doctrinal heritage.

Opportunities for Reflection

The following questions may be used by groups wishing to discuss the material in chapter one or by individuals wanting to reflect on issues raised within the chapter.

1. Richard Allen believed he could only be a Methodist. How important is denominational loyalty to you? Why are you a part of the United Methodist Church?

2. What parallels do you find between England in the 1800s and your twenty-first century experience? How might these similarities affect the United Methodist Church? How is your local congregation responding to these challenges and needs?

3. How important is it to know your family heritage in the formation of your personal identity? Are the same factors valid for knowing our Methodist heritage and how much does your local church emphasize its identity as United Methodist?

2

God Versus Idols

Beliefs Matter

I t makes no difference what you believe as long as you are sincere." Such a claim is often made in the name of faith and tolerance. The affirmation, which is itself a belief or tenet of faith, makes sincerity the criteria for religious devotion. It assumes that all religious beliefs are equal and their validity is judged by the firmness with which they are held and the sincerity with which they are acted upon. Truth becomes synonymous with strong conviction, and faithfulness is validated by "it feels right."

In a world of conflicting ideas, multiple faith options, competing loyalties, and the prevalence of violent religious extremism, minimizing the weight of religious beliefs has its appeal. Tough thinking and potentially divisive discernment become unnecessary. Furthermore, science and technology seemingly have rendered many religious concepts irrelevant. No longer do we depend upon religion to explain the world. Science provides answers to questions once considered the domain of religion. Modern developments in technology, economics, medicine, and politics provide solutions to problems once relegated to religious faith. In a world that defines truth as verifiable facts, religious beliefs seem to be merely speculative. As speculations and conjectures, they are held tentatively, awaiting empirical verification. Or, they are placed in a pious compartment of the mind isolated from the decisions and actions of everyday life. The religious beliefs themselves cease to matter. Only sincerity and tolerance matter.

Doctrine matters to Methodists! It serves three primary purposes. First, doctrines provide the basic framework for our view of life and of the world, what we call a "worldview." Through the lens of the historic affirmations of faith, we interpret and reflect on our own lives, the world around us, the past, and the future. Secondly, doctrine serves formational purposes. Doctrines are far more than abstract ideas and principles; they provide the foundation, motivation, and direction for our living; and the validity of a doctrine is judged by the character it produces in individuals and communities. Thirdly, doctrine serves an evangelical and apologetic purpose. Doctrine provides the basic content and core substance of our proclamation and defense of the Christian gospel. In 1786, John Wesley warned that Methodism would become "a dead sect" with the form of religion but lacking its power if its members failed to hold fast to doctrine, as well as the spirit and discipline with which the movement began.[1]

Indifferent to Doctrine?

A perception persists that "one can believe anything and be United Methodist." As stated in the introduction, such a characterization has deep roots in our history, though it represents a misreading of our tradition. As faithful Anglicans, Wesley and his colleagues presumed and affirmed the basic doctrines, beliefs, practices, and liturgies of the established church. The Articles of Religion, the *Book of Common Prayer*, and the Homilies of the Anglican Church formed the foundation of

Methodist beliefs. Wesley held tenaciously to the historic doctrines of the Christian faith and diligently proclaimed and taught them to the Methodists and the masses who heard him preach. That emphasis continued in America when the Methodists formed the Methodist Episcopal Church in 1784. A slightly modified version of the Articles of Religion of the Anglican Church and the Heidelberg Catechism of the Reformed tradition formed the bedrock of belief of the churches, which formed into the United Methodist Church.

Adding to the perception that Methodists are indifferent to doctrine is the emphasis upon current pluralism and diversity and its relationship to what Wesley called "catholic spirit." Wesley's commitment to "catholic spirit," or the oneness of the church in Jesus Christ, has often been misinterpreted to mean an indulgent indifference that makes sound doctrine subservient to tolerance. Further, Methodism's historic openness to diversity, its insistence on freedom to think and let think, and the belief that continuing exploration into the nature and purposes of God is a necessary component of faith have led some to assume that no doctrinal parameters exist. As The Book of Discipline states: "Wesley's familiar dictum was: 'As to all opinions which do not strike at the root of Christianity, we think and let think.'"[2]

However, although Wesley and the Methodists "were fully committed to the principles of religious toleration and theological diversity, they were equally confident that there is a 'marrow' of Christian truth that can be identified and that must be conserved."[3] Sound doctrine and catholic spirit are inseparable in the Wesleyan tradition as appropriate understanding of the nature and purposes of God results in "the love of God shed abroad in our hearts," thereby eschewing bigotry and rejection of those whose beliefs differ from ours.

The emphasis in all of the Methodist traditions has been on evangelization, holy living, and mission. Sound doctrine and refined beliefs were critical components of Methodism as a renewal movement. Wesley's challenge to the Church of England was not in the lack of clarity regarding basic Christian beliefs. It was the failure to live those beliefs. He sought to translate the doctrines from the realm of abstract thinking and compartmentalized creedal formulations into the worldview, proclamation, and character of the people called Methodists.

Beliefs Affect Living

Methodists take religious belief with the utmost seriousness as a way of viewing and living in the world. We know that beliefs shape behavior and practice. Beliefs and the stories that express them influence our self-image, our relationships, and our commitments. *The Book of Discipline* states: "No motif in the Wesleyan tradition has been more constant than the link between Christian doctrine and Christian living."[4]

Beliefs shape our self-image and our view of our own worth and destiny. It matters whether we consider ourselves worthless creatures or children of God, unredeemed sinners or forgiven disciples, hopeless victims of sin and death or citizens of an eternal kingdom. There is a vast difference in believing that our identity and worth are determined by our appearance, knowledge, and productivity and believing that we have infinite worth and dignity as sons and daughters of God.

Beliefs affect our relationships with others. It matters whether we see another person as an enemy or as a brother or sister; as inferior or as an equal; as a means to our ends or as a person for whom Christ died; as a criminal deserving of retribution or as a fellow sinner in need of forgiveness and restoration; as an object of our gratification or as a partner in a covenant.

Beliefs govern our relationship with the earth and its resources. It matters whether we see creation as a commodity to be exploited for human consumption or as God's household in which all creatures have access to God's abundance. It matters if we believe that the dominion given to human beings permits us to exploit and deplete the earth's resources or if the dominion bestowed on us is more like the responsibility of a shepherd to protect, nurture, and preserve the flock for the whole household and the next generation.

Beliefs form our understanding of and relationship with God. It matters whether we believe God is a cruel judge or a loving parent, an impersonal force or a personal friend, one who rules by coercive power and fear or one whose power is love. It matters if God is detached from the world and human experience or if God is present with the world and invites human beings to share in the divine life. It makes a difference if we believe God's preferential love and purposes are limited to our nation, our tribe, and our race, or if God's love and purposes include all humankind.

Practical Divinity

The Wesleyan emphasis is on "practical divinity." Wesley's primary concern was holy living, which is characterized by loving God and one's neighbor with Christ-like love. He wrote:

> I believe the merciful God regards the lives and tempers of men more than their ideas. I believe he respects the goodness of the heart rather than the clearness of the head; and that if the heart of a man be filled (by the grace of God, and the power of his Spirit) with the humble, gentle, patient love of God and man, God will not cast him into everlasting fire prepared for the devil and his angels because his ideas are not clear, or because his conceptions are confused. Without holiness, I own, no man shall see the Lord; but I dare not add, or clear ideas.[5]

The Methodist view of the primacy of holy living, however, is itself a significant belief. It is rooted in confidence in God's grace, which has the power to make us holy. It also results from the understanding of faith as acting upon the promises of God. Wesley knew from personal experience and observation that people act their way into believing as well as believe their way into acting. The Methodist emphasis upon "practical divinity" or holy living, therefore, recognizes the integral relationship between beliefs and behavior, faith and works. It is not a diminishing of the importance of beliefs; rather, it is a declaration of the importance of beliefs in shaping who we are and our relationship with God and the world.

A Conflict of Gods

A character in James Michener's *The Source* suffers the consequences of her husband's devotion to the wrong god. She grieves the loss of her son who was sacrificed to the god Melak. Now her husband celebrates the harvest by visiting the temple prostitute. Michener describes the woman's mood as she is obviously deeply pained by her husband's destructive behavior, which was influenced by his understanding of god. "And while others celebrated she walked slowly homeward, seeing life in a new and painful clarity: with different gods her husband . . . would have been a different man."[6]

We are shaped by our god(s). Whatever is ultimate to us is our god. As Martin Luther wrote, "Now, I say whatever your heart clings to and confides in, that is really your God."[7] Whatever we count on to give our lives meaning, purpose, value, and destiny is our god. Everyone, therefore, believes in something. We simply cannot survive without some value, person, story, ideas, or assumptions that give life coherent meaning and purpose.

The great conflicts are between competing gods, not between atheism and religion. Belief in a god is no virtue. Everybody believes in some god, some ultimate value(s). As far as we know, Jesus never met an atheist. It was belief in god(s) that resulted in people calling for Jesus to be crucified; and it was Jesus' belief in God which led him to pray from the cross, "Father, forgive them; for they know not what they do" (Luke 23:34, RSV). The religion of Saul of Tarsus led him to persecute followers of Jesus Christ, and Paul's faith in a different God led him to pen the words, "And now faith, hope, and love abide, these three; and the greatest of these is love" (1 Corinthians 13:13). The difference was in the nature of the God who shaped Paul's life. The nature of the God or gods we believe in and cling to is the critical issue.

Belief in god(s) accounts for some of history's most diabolical crimes, and belief in God explains history's most noble deeds. Adolf Hitler wrote in *Mein Kampf*: "Hence today I believe that I am acting in accordance with the will of the Almighty Creator: *by defending myself against the Jews, I am fighting for the work of the Lord.*"[8] The attempt to exterminate the Jews, a people defined by their faith in the God of the Exodus, was driven by a belief system that claimed loyalty to God. However, it was Dietrich Bonhoeffer's belief in God that caused him to give his life in an attempt to counter Hitler and Nazism. It was the belief that God had consigned some human beings to inferiority and servitude that supported the buying and selling of human beings as slaves; and it was the conviction that all persons are equal before God and loved infinitely by God that led others, including John Wesley, to consider slavery a sin against God and humanity.

A disparity often exists between the beliefs we consciously affirm and those on which we act. The gods that shape our lives and the God affirmed in our creeds are not always the same. Holding an intellectual belief in God falls short of having faith in God. Jesus distinguished between those who say "Lord, Lord" and those who do "the will of my Father" (Matthew 7:21, RSV). John Wesley once said that he had met only two atheists in the British Isles; however, he observed that many "Christians" live "without God in the world." Those who profess belief in God but act without reference to God Wesley called "practical atheists."[9]

Jean-Paul Sartre, a philosopher who has influenced modern thinking about religion, writes: "Existentialism isn't so atheistic that it wears itself out showing that God doesn't exist. Rather, it declares that even if God did exist, that would change nothing."[10] Many people believe in God in the same way they believe in the existence of life on other planets: There may be such a thing, but it makes no difference in how they live. They are practical atheists. Or, more accurately, they affirm the possible existence of God but other gods shape their lives.

Multiple gods compete for our loyalty. Polytheism (belief in many gods) and idolatry are as prevalent among modern church members as they were among the ancient Canaanites. We feel torn by conflicting values. It is difficult to act with singleness of motive and commitment. Maintaining belief in the God who is concerned about, present with, and working for the healing of creation is not easy. Being shaped by the God present as Father, Son, and Holy Spirit demands considerable discernment and intentionality in today's world.

Popular Rivals to the God of Jesus Christ

Seldom is idolatry an explicit and intentional following of gods other than the one in which we affirm belief. If our god is whatever "our hearts cling to" and whatever shapes our living, then we may identify our idols by asking: What really determines my decisions and actions? What is of supreme importance to me? What realities mold and shape my life? What does my heart cling to? For most of us, the answers are complex. Many ideas, relationships, values, stories, and goals influence us. We are not even conscious of all that shapes us. Seldom do we identify the reasons for our being, behaving, or believing. Much of the motivation is subconscious or unknown. Who we are and what we do result from multiple cultural, family, and personal realities.

Few people in our society consciously and explicitly reject the God revealed in the Exodus and in Jesus Christ. However, few people—if any—can claim to be shaped totally by such a God. Being shaped by the God of our creeds is very difficult and rare today. God has many appealing and subtle rivals. Here are a few of the gods that influence all of us.

SUCCESS

Success defined as achieving, accumulating, and receiving applause is a popular god. The temptation to center our lives in what we own, or know, or can do is pervasive. Our society tends to value people in terms of their possessions, titles, looks, educational degrees, economic productivity, and professional or political power. Competition is valued above cooperation. Winning and advancing consume our energy and resources as individuals and institutions. Right and wrong are determined by what contributes to success. People become instruments or stepping stones to achievement. Personal well-being and national security are calculated by ranking.

The Bible invites us to be shaped by a different God than success. Jesus warned that "many who are first will be last, and the last will be first" (Matthew 19:30). He challenged us to find life by losing it (Matthew 10:37-39) and to avoid seeking the "chief seats." According to Jesus, the meek shall inherit the earth (Matthew 5:5). Greatness is in serving rather than being served. "Life does not consist in the abundance of possessions," he affirmed (Luke 12:15). His own temptation in the wilderness was a struggle with the success god as he defeated the tempter's challenge to root his life in prestige, popularity, and political power (Matthew 4:1-11).

CONSUMERISM

The market economy and its accompanying consumerism is perhaps the most pervasive god of the twenty-first century. Economics and the global market have become foundational and determinative, the lens through which life is viewed and practiced. This god considers everything a commodity to be marketed and consumed. Dr. Douglas Meeks is one Wesleyan scholar who contends that the market logic is the dominant idol of our time.[11] The logic of the market puts prime value on exchange and utility. Worth depends on the exchange value in the market and the contribution to the economy. Things, persons, institutions, and relationships are reduced to their utilitarian function. Relationships are evaluated based on what one receives from them.

Vincent J. Miller in *Consuming Religion: Christian Faith and Practice in a Consumerist Culture* emphasizes that culture itself has become a commodity—the arts, education, labor, natural resources, entertainment, and religion. When religion becomes a commodity, its beliefs, liturgies, stories, symbols, and institutions are severed from their original intention and basic narrative.[12] They become marketing tools for institutional or personal enhancement or commodities to be consumed for utilitarian benefit.

Consumerism reduces even God to a commodity to be used as a solution to personal problems or a means to selfish ends. God is portrayed as an instrument of one's happiness, success, and peace of mind rather than as One who invites us to participate in God's reign of compassion, justice, righteousness, and joy. Laurence Moore, Professor of History at Cornell University, contends that what we usually mean by secularization has to do not so much with the disappearance of religion but its commodification.[13] That is, religion has ceased to be the basic framework or logic through which we view the world. Instead, religion has become another optional commodity in which we participate depending upon our choices and how well it meets our self-identified needs.

Commodification reduces the doctrines, language, rituals, symbols, and practices of religion to their utilitarian function. Religion becomes an option among multiple options in the marketplace of products offering self-actualization, fulfillment, success, relief from suffering, and immortality. Profound symbols become trinkets or adornments, part of the advertising, or rhetoric by which we sell economically driven agendas.

Much in the contemporary church reflects the idolatry of consumerism. Many people join the church simply because of what it has to offer them. A "gospel of prosperity" replaces the radical and costly good news of God's new creation in Jesus Christ. Churches become competitors vying for a greater share of the religious market. Evangelism is reduced to a marketing strategy for the recruitment of members rather than the proclamation of the good news of God's redemptive action in Jesus Christ. Worship is evaluated based on its ability to attract the masses rather than being an offering the worshiper brings to God. Discipleship and mission become options in the church's schedule of multiple options, including recreation and entertainment. A church's faithfulness is judged by its size and how it meets the self-defined needs of its participants rather than being judged by how closely it fulfills its mission to be a visible sign and instrument of God's reign in Jesus Christ.

Consumerism runs counter to belief in God as the Creator and human beings as stewards. If this is "my Father's world" then we are responsible to God for our participation in creation. Since God desires that all creation live in harmony and all persons be treated with justice and compassion, there is a higher standard than individual needs or desires that masquerade as needs. As the sovereign of creation, God is to be worshipped and served. We are means to God's ends, not the reverse. The church exists to fulfill God's mission rather than to further our narcissistic goals. Jesus warned, "For what will it profit them to gain the whole world and forfeit their life?" (Mark 8:36). He defined authentic life in terms of the willingness to give it up and declared that discipleship includes the willingness to "sell all that you own and distribute the money to the poor" (Luke 18:18-25, also see Luke 14:33).

Wesley considered the accumulation of wealth and consumerism to be perhaps the most serious threats to the Christian gospel in general and to the Methodist movement in particular. His famous sermon "On the Use of Money"[14] is a call to avoid consumerism by adopting a simple lifestyle and giving to the poor. He believed that becoming a Christian makes one diligent and frugal, which in turn tends to result in growing wealthier. He contended that as people increase in riches they decrease in grace. They become distracted from the pursuit of holiness of heart and life, assume a stance of self-sufficiency, and separate themselves from the poor. In order to avoid the temptations of consumerism and wealth, early Methodists were urged to build plain meeting houses, limit their expenditures only to the necessities, and give the remainder to the poor. For Wesley, anything we have that is superfluous is a form of robbery of the poor. The early Methodists believed that sharing in the life of the self-giving God of Jesus meant sharing in the life of the poor and avoiding the seduction of consumerism.

HEDONISM

Hedonism is another popular god that molds and shapes our lives. *Webster's New Collegiate Dictionary* defines hedonism as "the doctrine that pleasure or happiness is the sole or chief good in life."[15] The pursuit of pleasure, the avoidance of struggle, and the attainment of peace of mind become the primary goals. Right and wrong depend upon feelings. "If it feels good, do it." Or, "It must be right if it feels right." Ethics and morality become a matter of subjectivity and personal choice. Relationships, beliefs, and activities are judged by their ability to bring pleasure and make one happy. God is reduced to a facilitator of good feelings, a celestial "Dr. Phil," a means of avoiding suffering and struggle, and a champion of personal happiness. The church becomes a religious spa, the effectiveness of which is judged by its ability to solve personal problems and create positive feelings.

The Bible and our Wesleyan tradition emphasize happiness. In the Beatitudes of Jesus (Matthew 5:1-12) "blessed" can be translated "happy." Jesus' definition of happiness, however, represents a contrast to hedonism. The Bible considers happiness as a serendipity, a by-product of a life shared with the God of Jesus Christ. Happiness results from commitment to Jesus Christ who said, ". . . whoever does not take up the cross and follow me is not worthy of me. Those who find their life will lose it, and those who lose their life for my sake will find it" (Matthew 10:38-39).

John Wesley often coupled happiness with holiness. Wesley considered happiness a dimension of true religion. He proclaimed, "But true religion, or a heart right toward God and man, implies happiness as well as holiness."[16] But he claimed that there is no happiness apart from holiness; and holiness is the result of sharing in God's righteousness. He wrote, "This holiness and happiness, joined in one, are sometimes styled in the inspired writings, 'the kingdom of God' . . . because it is the immediate fruit of God's reigning in the soul."[17] Happiness in the Wesleyan tradition, then, is the by-product of our relationship with God, the participation in God's reign of justice, compassion, righteousness, and joy. Only those who "strive first for the kingdom of God and his righteousness" (Matthew 6:33) have authentic happiness as a serendipity of commitment.

Among other popular gods which are shaping our lives are nationalism, the worship of the nation; individualism, which extols the individual to the detriment of the community; rationalism, which exalts reason to the extreme by disallowing revelation and mystery; racism and sexism, which assign worth according to race and gender and use power to maintain one's own privileged position; violence, which considers that 'might makes right' and relies upon violence for security and self-esteem; and institutional religion, which confines God's presence and activity to religious institutions and gives religious rituals and doctrines priority over justice, mercy, and compassion.

Popular Gods Distort Reality and Thwart Abundant Life

Idolatry distorts reality, robs us of abundant life, and thwarts God's plan for the world. It is instructive that in the listings of the Ten Commandments, the first reads, "I am the Lord your God, who brought you out of the land of Egypt, out of the house of slavery; you shall have no other gods before me" (Exodus 20:2; Deuteronomy 5:6). The idols of success, consumerism, hedonism, nationalism, individualism, rationalism, racism and sexism, violence, and institutional religion distort reality, destroy creation and community, and create enormous suffering. Such idols are causing the deaths of millions of people each year from poverty. Idolatry is killing millions by violence and depleting the earth's resources. Although adequate resources exist to provide for the basic needs for food, shelter, education, medical care, and clothing to all people on earth, the pursuit of false gods is resulting in millions of God's children being deprived of those necessities.

It matters which God or gods one believes in, and whatever shapes our lives is truly our god (God). The problem with idols is that they distort reality, rob life of its ultimate meaning, and finally destroy life itself. They cut us off from the true God, in whose reign we and all people are invited to participate. It is important, therefore, that we "not believe every spirit, but test the spirits to see whether they are from God" (1 John 4:1). As one United Methodist theologian reminds us, "To believe in God is at once to disbelieve what is not of God."[18]

Conclusion

Beliefs matter! They shape us. Our relationships with one another and with the earth itself are grounded in our assumptions, our values, our dreams, and our perceptions. Whatever molds our lives is our God. The God we affirm in our creeds is not always the God that shapes our lives. The relationship between beliefs and behavior is complex and multifaceted. Integrity requires compatibility between our creeds and deeds.

John Wesley argued that true religion includes correct doctrine and faithful practices. But it is more! At the heart of Christian doctrine and practice is love of God and neighbor made possible by grace. He wrote, "The nature of religion is so far from consisting in these, in forms of worship, or rites and ceremonies, that it does not properly consist in any outward actions of what kind so ever."[19] He adds, "For neither does religion consist in orthodoxy or right opinions; . . . A man may be orthodox in every point; he may not only espouse right opinions, but zealously defend them against all opposers; he may think justly concerning the incarnation of our Lord, concerning the ever blessed Trinity, and every other doctrine contained in the oracles of God" and still not be authentically religious.[20] Wesley proceeded to define true religion as loving God with all the heart, and with all the mind, and with all the soul, and with all the strength, and loving one's neighbor as one's self.

Authentic religion for the Methodists means sharing the life of God whose love is poured out in Jesus Christ and whose Holy Spirit shapes us into the likeness of Christ and empowers us to be holy as God is holy. Religion, then, is a relationship with a particular God, the One we call Trinity. The character in James Michener's book knew the importance of belief in God. The husband would be a different man if he had a different god. Who is the God revealed in Jesus Christ and witnessed to in the Bible, the historic creeds, and the experience of the church? It is to that question we now turn.

Opportunities for Reflection

The following questions may be used by groups wishing to discuss the material in chapter two or by individuals wanting to reflect on issues raised within the chapter.

1. James Michener's character said of her husband, "He would be a different man had he a different god." What differences does your belief in the God of the Bible make in your life?

2. How do you understand John Wesley's statement, "As to all opinions which do not strike at the root of Christianity, we think and let think"? How comfortable are you with this statement?

3. This chapter discusses how we are shaped by values and ideas. What ideas or values influence and shape you? Do some values compete for your loyalty to God? What indications do you see of the idols of success, consumerism, hedonism, nationalism, etc.?

4. What are some recent destructive events resulting from belief in God or gods? What are some positive contributions of belief in God in the contemporary world?

3

The God Whose Life We Share

In the book *Night*, Elie Wiesel shares his experiences as a young prisoner in Nazi concentration camps. The anguish, suffering, and death experienced by Wiesel challenge the reader's confidence in the existence of a loving God. A fellow prisoner raised the basic religious question during the hanging of three people, including a child. The prisoners in the camp were all forced to march past the gallows and watch the youngster die. He had a face like an angel. Since his body was small, it took him longer to die. As the prisoners watched this barbaric, senseless, dastardly spectacle of a child struggling between life and death, someone asked, "Where is God?" Expressing his despair about God's apparent absence, Wiesel thought: "Where is He? Here He is—He is hanging here on this gallows. . . ."[1]

Who and Where Is God?

Amid a world where suffering and death are universally present, the questions are inevitable and necessary: Who is God? Where is God? What is God doing, if anything? Such questions express the longing within the human spirit for some transcendent presence and meaning. Television daily brings anguished scenes of traumatic suffering into our homes. Needless starvation, unnecessary poverty, senseless violence and incurable diseases challenge our belief in a God who is both powerful and compassionate. Where is God? Surely God is other than the one who simply views the human tragedy from a detached distance.

Doubt is sometimes the most honest and authentic affirmation of faith. Questioning is a gift of God by which we "test the spirits to see whether they are from God" (1 John 4:1). The poet Tennyson wrote:

There is more faith in honest doubt,
Believe me, than in half the creeds.[2]

Questions about the nature, purposes, and presence of God run throughout Holy Scripture. Job's anguished cries in the midst of undeserved suffering and tragedy are expressions of faith as well as doubt: "Oh, that I knew where I might find him . . .!" (23:3). "What is the Almighty, that we should serve him? And what profit do we get if we pray to him?" (21:15). The Psalms contain more laments than praise as the Psalmists bare their souls to God: "How long, O Lord? Will you forget me forever? How long will you hide your face from me?" (13:1); or "O Lord, why do you cast me off? Why do you hide your face from me?" (86:14). Jesus, reciting Psalm 22, cried from the cross, "My God, my God, why have you forsaken me?" (Matthew 27:46).

Since much of the world's needless suffering has roots in religion, questions about the nature, presence, and purposes of God belong at the center of religious reflection and devotion. Through faith, expressed in doubt and confrontation with the scarred hands and side of the crucified and risen Christ, the Apostle Thomas was able to declare with new understanding, "My Lord and my God!" (John 20:28).

Atheism has gained increased attention in the public media in recent years with books by such prominent and thoughtful intellectuals as Sam Harris, Christopher Hitchens, and Richard Dawkins.[3]

They rightly point out the terrible and destructive manifestations of religion in the modern world and present challenges that must be taken seriously by those of us whose worldview and behavior are grounded in faith in God. However, belief in God is not the substantive issue. It is the kind of God one believes in and trusts, and we must persistently and humbly evaluate our own understanding of God in the light of scripture, the historic creeds, and the continuing revelation of the Holy Spirit within the Christian community.

THE GOD WE KNOW AS TRINITY

The United Methodist doctrinal/theological statement affirms: "With Christians of other communions we confess belief in the triune God—Father, Son, and Holy Spirit. This confession embraces the biblical witness to God's activity in creation, encompasses God's gracious self-involvement in the dramas of history, and anticipates the consummation of God's reign."[4] It is the Trinity—Father, Son, and Holy Spirit—that provides our grounding for knowing and relating to God.

For Christians, the ambiguous word "God" comes into specific focus in the Triune name and in the cross, where the questions "Who is God?" and "Where is God?" are answered with shattering clarity. The Trinity is the narrative description of God who is a communion of love and freedom into which we are invited to participate. It is the framework for understanding the nature, character, purposes, and presence of God. At its core meaning is this declaration: God, the Father, who is before us; God, the Son, who is for us; God, the Holy Spirit, who is with us.

Faith is more than intellectual abstractions about God. Faith is fundamentally a relationship with God—a loving and reverent relationship of trustful obedience. Faith in God is *living* in relationship with God. Inquiry into God and relationship with God, however, do not take place in a vacuum or without resources. It is a primary affirmation that God has taken the initiative to disclose the divine character, action, and presence. God has responded to our longings, questions, and doubts. Jesus Christ, as witnessed to in scripture and in the church, understood through reason and experience, and in whose life and ministry we share through the Holy Spirit, is God's answer to the question, "Where is God now?"

JESUS CHRIST, GOD FOR US

Central to the Christian faith is the conviction that Jesus Christ is the supreme revelation of God. Our doctrinal statement affirms:

> At the heart of the gospel of salvation is God's incarnation in Jesus of Nazareth. Scripture witnesses to the redeeming love of God in Jesus' life and teachings, his atoning death, his resurrection, his sovereign presence in history, his triumph over the powers of evil and death, and his promised return. . . .
>
> Through faith in Jesus Christ we are forgiven, reconciled to God, and transformed as people of the new covenant.[5]

Jesus Christ is the very flesh and blood of God's nature and God's intention for all humanity. Jesus of Nazareth is the human face and action of the Father, and is Creator of the universe made known in history. John's Gospel proclaims, "And the Word became flesh and lived among us, and we have seen his glory, the glory as of a father's only son, full of grace and truth. . . . From his fullness we have all received, grace upon grace" (John 1:14, 16). Charles Wesley's beloved Christmas hymn expresses the Church's understanding of Jesus Christ:

> Christ, by highest heaven adored;
> Christ, the everlasting Lord,
> late in time behold him come,
> off-spring of a virgin's womb.
>
> Veiled in flesh the God-head see;
> hail th'incarnate Deity,
> pleased with us in flesh to dwell,
> Jesus, our Emmanuel.[6]

People who join The United Methodist Church are asked to accept Jesus Christ as Lord and Savior. He is both "the everlasting Lord" and "our Emmanuel." Accepting Jesus Christ as Lord means to live in terms of the sovereignty of Christ over all creation. As the revelation of God and God's purpose for humanity, Jesus Christ merits our full devotion, loyalty, and confidence. His life, teachings, death, resurrection, and ascension are the ultimate source of our understanding of ourselves, other people, the world, and the meaning and destiny of life. As the embodiment of the Everlasting God, the Creator of heaven and earth, Jesus Christ can be trusted, obeyed, and followed.

When asked what it means to accept Jesus Christ as Lord, a youth responded, "It means Jesus is the boss." Jesus Christ is more than "the boss," the one to be obeyed. Accepting Jesus as Lord means that we trust who he is, do what he says to do, go where he goes, welcome those whom he loves, and live toward his promises. The initial invitation to the first disciples was "Follow me." The invitation was not primarily to follow a set of rules or to believe certain doctrines. It was an invitation to a relationship—a transforming friendship. The one who is Lord—Sovereign—is also Savior. He is the one who enables us to be and do that which he commands and who accompanies us toward the fulfillment of his promises.

In Jesus Christ, God entered the human struggle with sin and death, which thwart the divine intention for life. In the crucifixion, Jesus confronted and absorbed the consequences and power of sin and death. The cross represents the results of sin and suffering and God's response to them. Christ on the cross gives new meaning to Elie Wiesel's declaration of despair, "There God is, on the gallows." God is not absent! God has taken on the powers of evil and sin and God has won! The resurrection of Jesus Christ is God's eternal and resounding "no!" to the principalities and powers of darkness. The ascension of the risen Christ is God's promise to complete the victory begun in Jesus Christ. As we affirm in The Great Thanksgiving during Holy Communion, "Christ has died; Christ is risen; Christ will come again."[7]

Because Jesus Christ has entered the struggle with sin and death, and emerges triumphant, we can face our own sin and death with forgiveness and hope. Because God has won the ultimate victory, nothing in all creation is able to separate us from the love of God in Christ Jesus our Lord (Romans 8:39). In the power of the Holy Spirit, through baptism, we are incorporated into the death and resurrection of Jesus Christ and become part of the new humanity God is creating. We have been made brothers and sisters of Christ and one another. The God who is for us in Jesus Christ has grafted us into the Divine life and mission and is forever with us in the Holy Spirit.

THE HOLY SPIRIT, GOD WITH US

United Methodists affirm in "A Modern Affirmation":

> We believe in the Holy Spirit
> as the divine presence in our lives,
> whereby we are kept in remembrance
> of the truth of Christ,
> and find strength and help in time of need.[8]

The Holy Spirit is God with us to comfort and convict, to remind and renew, to guide and guard, to sustain and support. Through the work of the Holy Spirit, we are convicted of our sin and assured of forgiveness. We are reminded of Jesus Christ and renewed in our relationship, guided toward the fulfillment of God's purposes, and guarded against the powers of sin and death. In the power of the Holy Spirit we are sustained and supported amid temptation, suffering, and death. It is the Holy Spirit who draws us toward God and into community with God and one another.

As one United Methodist scholar writes, "The Spirit is represented as the linking up of the life span of Jesus Christ, the incarnate Word, with our own life span."[9] The test of whether a spirit is the Holy Spirit is its conformity to Jesus Christ (1 John 4:2ff). The fruits of the Spirit are the qualities of Jesus' own being: "love, joy, peace, patience, kindness, generosity, faithfulness, gentleness, and self-control" (Galatians 5:22). Such qualities within and among human beings are God with us; they are not human achievements or universal "natural" characteristics. What we cannot produce in ourselves God produces in us—faith, hope, and love or Christ-likeness. Christopher Morse states it well: "By the indwelling of the Holy Spirit, and not by any alleged self-actualization of our own spirits, we relate to others in ways that result in freedom and communion."[10]

The Holy Spirit is a gift that the God who is for us in Jesus Christ bestows upon us. At Pentecost, the Spirit broke down the barriers between human beings, loosened the tongues of the apostles, and brought into being a new community. The Holy Spirit began shaping a community after the likeness of Jesus Christ and empowering it to be a sign, foretaste, and instrument of Christ's final victory. It is into that community, the church, that the Holy Spirit incorporates us. Through the guidance and strength of the Holy Spirit, the church becomes the "body of Christ" in mission to the world.

A hymn by Brian Foley prayerfully expresses the meaning and power of the Holy Spirit. It begins:

Holy Spirit, come, confirm us in the truth that Christ makes known;
we have faith and understanding through your helping gifts alone. [11]

THE FATHER, GOD BEFORE US

For more than sixteen hundred years, Christians have declared in the words of The Apostles' Creed: "I believe in God the Father Almighty, maker of heaven and earth . . ." The first of the Methodist Articles of Religion reads, "There is but one living and true God, everlasting, without body or parts, of infinite power, wisdom, and goodness; the maker and preserver of all things, both visible and invisible. And in unity of this Godhead there are three persons, of one substance, power, and eternity—the Father, the Son, and the Holy Spirit." [12]

The God who is for us in Jesus Christ and with us in the Holy Spirit is also before us as the Creator of heaven and earth. The mighty acts of salvation in Jesus Christ into which we are incorporated through the Holy Spirit have their origin in the One who brought creation into being. The One by whose power Mary conceived a Son is the One whose "wind swept over the face of the waters" and formed the earth out of the "formless void and darkness" (Genesis 1:2). The Power who brought forth Jesus Christ from the death and darkness of the tomb also called forth creation from chaos and nothingness. The One who created the heavens and the earth, redeemed and reconciled all things in Jesus Christ, and is present with us is bringing a new heaven and a new earth through the power of the Holy Spirit.

Since all creation has its origin and destiny in God, everything is dependent and contingent upon God. The highest value of any part of creation lies in the purpose assigned to it by the Creator. Human beings are stewards, cultivators, nurturers, and preservers of creation. God the Creator has invited us to share in the divine creativity and in ongoing efforts to bring healing and wholeness to creation, now scarred and wounded by human sin and continuing chaos.

The affirmation of God as Father is not a declaration of God's gender. It is a statement about God's power, which brings all creation into being and the quality of God's relationship with creation, especially human beings. God is neither male nor female; God is "without body or parts." However, the Creator is not an impersonal or detached power, like electricity. God is personally and intimately involved with that which is created, like a mother and father with their children, or an artist with her painting, or a potter with his clay.

The Suffering God

Amid the grotesque cruelty and traumatic suffering of World War II, a German pastor and theologian, Dietrich Bonhoeffer, was hanged in a Nazi concentration camp. Before his death, Bonhoeffer wrote, "The Bible directs man to God's powerlessness and suffering; only the suffering God can help."[13] That is precisely the distinguishing and defining quality of the God of the Bible. God the Father, the Son, and the Holy Spirit is a suffering God who feels the pain and anguish of the world and its people. In the Exodus and in the cross, God is revealed as both Liberator and Suffering Servant who sees the misery of the people, hears their cries on account of their taskmasters, experiences their sufferings, and comes to deliver (Exodus 3:7-8). In the words of the philosopher Alfred North Whitehead: "God is the Great Companion—the fellow sufferer who understands."[14]

A unique characteristic of the God of the Bible is vulnerability to suffering, grief, and anguish. Whereas the gods of other cultures and religions were viewed as invincible and removed from the sufferings of the world, the God of the Hebrew Scriptures and the New Testament is portrayed as One who enters the sufferings of people. In fact, God is revealed as having an especially close relationship with those who suffer and are oppressed. God chooses the least—the most vulnerable, the powerless—as special messengers and means of accomplishing divine purposes. When a community was chosen to be a "light to the nations" (Isaiah 49:6), it was a band of powerless slaves. The chosen leaders were most often the youngest—the least prominent. The welfare and well-being of the chosen ones depended upon their executing justice and compassion for God's special friends—the poor, orphans, widows, sojourners, and strangers.

When God entered human flesh, it was as a vulnerable baby, born of a young peasant mother. His first bed was a cattle stall. He was among the homeless. He spent the first months of his young life with his family as an alien in Egypt. He grew up in a working-class family and provided for the family by working with his hands in a carpenter's shop. When he began his public ministry, he called ordinary folks as disciples. The purpose of his ministry was announced as "to bring good news to the poor . . . to proclaim release to the captives and recovery of sight to the blind, to let the oppressed go free, to proclaim the year of the Lord's favor" (Luke 4:18-19). He so closely identified with the poor, the imprisoned, and the sick that "just as you did it to one of the least of these . . . you did it to me" (Matthew 25:40).

This Messiah of God associated with outcasts, the sick, the poor, the disreputable, women, and children. He healed the sick, fed the hungry, raised the dead, wept with a grieving family, touched the untouchable lepers, pronounced forgiveness to the sinful, restored sight to the blind, blessed children, challenged the self-righteous, prayed for his executioners, and died among thieves. This is God for us, God with us, and God before us!

Where is God now? "There God is on the gallows!" God suffers both as the Son crucified and as the Father who enters the pain of a crucified and beloved child.

What is God doing? God is sharing the suffering, grief, anguish, and death of the world—and working to overcome it. God as the Holy Spirit is working to bring healing, reconciliation, and wholeness to all creation. Therefore, we can face our own and the world's suffering, sin, and death with confidence, knowing that the crucified and risen God is for us and with us, and goes before us.

Conclusion

The writer of Ephesians issues the gospel's most important challenge: "Therefore be imitators of God, as beloved children, and live in love, as Christ loved us and gave himself up for us, a fragrant offering and sacrifice to God" (Ephesians 5:1).

As we affirmed in chapter two, the greatest threat to Christian discipleship is not atheism; it is idolatry, being shaped by and imitating the wrong god(s). Many gods compete for our loyalty and devotion. They capture our attention and shape our lives sometimes without our awareness and conscious permission. Gradually, we take on the nature of the god in whom we trust. Therefore, the kind of god we trust is crucial.

We have been created to live in communion with God, a particular God: God the Father, the Son, and the Holy Spirit. The God whose life we share is before us as the Creator on whom all life depends and toward whose new creation all life will be judged. In Jesus Christ, God became incarnate and triumphed through and over suffering, sin, and death. This same God is present with us as the Holy Spirit to comfort, convict, guide, support, and sustain.

The last words of John Wesley prior to his death on March 2, 1791, at the age of nearly eighty-eight were, "The best of all, God is with us."[15] The day before, the weak and feeble leader of the Methodist movement began singing Isaac Watts' hymn, "I'll praise my Maker while I've breath." This was a favorite hymn of Wesley and he included it in his very first hymnbook—the 1737 Collection of Psalms and Hymns—and it appeared in every major hymn collection he published through his life. The hymn describes the appropriate response to the God who had shaped Wesley's life and ministry among the people called Methodist:

I'll praise my Maker while I've breath,
and when my voice is lost in death,
praise shall employ my nobler powers.

My days of praise shall ne'er be past,
while life, and thought, and being last,
or immortality endures.

Happy are they whose hopes rely
on Israel's God, who made the sky
and earth and seas, with all their train;

whose truth forever stands secure,
who saves th'oppressed and feeds the poor,
for none shall find God's promise vain.

The Lord pours eyesight on the blind;
the Lord supports the fainting mind
and sends the laboring conscience peace.

God helps the stranger in distress,
the widow and the fatherless,
and grants the prisoner sweet release.

I'll praise my God who lends me breath;
and when my voice is lost in death
praise shall employ my nobler powers.

My days of praise shall ne'er be past,
while life, and thought, and being last,
or immortality endures.[16]

Opportunities for Reflection

The following questions may be used by groups wishing to discuss the material in chapter three or by individuals wanting to reflect on issues raised within the chapter.

1. When have you experienced doubt about the existence, nature, or presence of God? How do you respond to the quotation from Tennyson: "There is more faith in honest doubt, believe me, than in half the creeds"?

2. What difference does your faith in the Triune God make in how you live?

3. Do you have friends/acquaintances who are atheists? How do you share your belief in God with someone who does not profess such belief?

4. Do you agree with Bonhoeffer's statement, "The Bible directs [man] to God's powerlessness and suffering; only the suffering God can help." Why? Why not?

5. What are the implications of God's special friendship/relationship with the poor, the suffering, the vulnerable, and the outcasts?

6. Where have you experienced the presence of God within the last few days? What makes you believe it was God whom you experienced?

4

Made in God's Image

Our beliefs about the nature, purposes, and activity of God shape and mold our lives. The kind of God we believe in and trust makes all the difference in how we live; and the doctrine of the Trinity is more than an abstract belief; it is a way of living in the world. All existence is redefined by trust in the Triune God, who is for us in Jesus Christ, before us as Father/ Creator, and with us in the Holy Spirit. Commitment to the God who enters into suffering humanity and triumphs over sin and death transforms our understanding of ourselves and of our world. Faithfulness requires that we persistently raise the critical questions: Who is God? Where is God? What is God doing?

Questions of equal importance are: Who are we as human beings? Does our life have meaning? If so, what is the purpose of human existence? What is our appropriate relationship to God and the creation of which we are part? How does our identity in relationship with God affect how we live and how we relate to others and the creation? The ancient psalmist raised the issue this way:

> When I look at your heavens, the work of your fingers,
> the moon and stars that you have established;
> what are human beings that you are mindful of them,
> mortals that you care for them? (Psalm 8:3-4)

What we believe about the nature and purpose of human beings matters! Psychologists validate the importance of self-image in the formation of our identity and behavior. The role of anthropology (our understanding of human beings) in shaping society has been documented by sociology. How we treat ourselves and others—and how we form communities and nations—is determined by the image we have of human beings. It matters what we believe about the worth, value, purpose, and destiny of these creatures whom the psalmist declared God made "a little lower than God, and crowned them with glory and honor" (Psalm 8:5).

The Christian faith, as understood and practiced by United Methodists, affirms that our identity as human beings is derived from the Triune God. Through the eternal Word in the power of the Holy Spirit, God has given us an identity that transcends biology, economics, or politics. We have been created in the *imago Dei* ("image of God"), redeemed in Jesus Christ, and incorporated into the body of Christ. As creatures made in the divine image by grace, human beings have been gifted with infinite worth, dignity, and destiny. Our identity lies in the One to whom we belong and in whose image we are made, not in how we look, what we know, or what we can do. God has created, redeemed, and claimed us as adopted children who participate in the divine presence and activity in the world. Therein lies our identity, worth, mission, and destiny!

This has been a distinctive emphasis of Methodism from its inception. John Wesley's first university sermon, preached in St. Mary's, the university church at Oxford, on November 15, 1730, was based on Genesis 1:27: "So God created man in his own image" (RSV).[1] This basic biblical affirmation formed the foundation of Wesley's doctrine of the "way of salvation" as the primary agenda of Christian living. The understanding of human beings as bearing the divine image helped to account for the Methodists' success among the poor and marginalized who had been stripped of their dignity and worth by alternative understandings. It is a message desperately needed in the impersonal and impoverished world of the twenty-first century.

The affirmation that God's grace is universal and that human beings have their basic origin in God makes political, geographic, ideological, and even religious distinctions subordinate to our common identity as creatures made in the divine image. John Wesley cautioned Methodists against bigotry, which he defined as ". . . too strong an attachment to, or fondness for, our own party, opinion, Church, and religion."[2] Bigotry originates in the elevation of any distinction—political, ethnic, religious—above God's universal grace which creates humanity in the divine image.

Alternative Understandings of Human Beings

That the Creator of the heavens and the earth would bestow upon humans the status of being "a little less than God" was a source of astonishment and inspiration to the ancient psalmist. In the world of eighteenth-century England, the message that human beings were created in the image of the divine helped to spark a moral and religious revival. In a world now dominated by science, economics, and politics, such a lofty status ascribed to humans is exaggerated by some and denied by others.

It is not self-evident that humans are created in the divine image and share in the life of God. Sufficient evidence exists to support the notion that human beings are created in the likeness of the demonic. While standing in front of the gallows in a Nazi death camp watching a child die, Elie Wiesel could have asked in addition to "Where is God?"[3] the corollary question, "Where is humanity?" Senseless violence, needless poverty, widespread exploitation, calloused cruelty, and the impersonal nature of modern life point to the absence of the divine image in the creatures the psalmist identifies as a little less than God.

Scientific developments and emerging economic and political trends raise new questions about the status and role of human beings. Humanity's distinctiveness in sharing God's life has been eroding for at least three hundred years. The astronomy of Galileo, Copernicus, and Newton challenged the notion that the earth is the center of the solar system. The prevailing idea of an enclosed creation with the earth as central has been replaced with a universe of infinite space and unfathomable distances. The earth has been reduced to a small planet among countless planets in a constellation of numberless galaxies. So the poet's wonder is compounded: "When I look at your heavens . . . the moon and stars . . . what are human beings . . . ?" (Psalm 8:3-4). In such a vast and limitless universe, it is not easy to believe that God notices a sparrow's fall and counts the hairs on our head (Luke 12:6-7).

We live amid a biological as well as cosmological revolution and we are tempted to reduce human beings to their biological components. Human beings are biological creatures. Many characteristics that identify us and distinguish us from one another are biological—skin color, gender, height, weight, facial features, physical stamina and health, brain capacity, and many personality traits. Behavior, attitudes, and perceptions have biological roots. Unknown and predetermined genetic influences help to shape our identity. We are, indeed, complex, interrelated biological organisms—a multifaceted composite of biological, chemical, environmental, and social realities.

As human beings, we are part of an intricate web of biological life. John Wesley suggested that human beings are part of a chain of being that includes the entire created order. He expressed the view that animals too have "souls" and will be part of God's final saving work as God redeems all that God loves.[4] Modern biology validates our kinship with other species. More than 98 percent of the molecules that make up the human being are shared by other species. A biologist said to me, "We human beings have no reason to boast; we are only recycled atoms. The atoms in us have been in beasts, plants, birds, animals, and reptiles." Therefore, reason exists to question the traditional species' chauvinism that has motivated the human exploitation of creation. Human kinship with all other creatures is now irrefutable and such kinship challenges the notion that humans are "created a little lower than the angels." Even the psalmist, however, reminds us that we are "dust," and, "As for mortals, their days are like grass; they flourish like a flower of the field; for the wind passes over it, and it is gone . . ." (Psalm 103:15-16).

The identification and manipulation of the approximately one hundred thousand genes in the human cell pose new questions about the extent of human freedom and the source of human worth and identity. The ability of scientists to create, duplicate, modify, and terminate life challenges the traditional religious understanding of life as a gift of a sovereign God in whose hands rest our beginning and end.

Is that the total picture? Are human beings to be defined, valued, or treated primarily in terms of their biological qualities? Is the human being to be reduced to a complex machine with multiple parts? Do genes and atoms decide our destiny? Are we to be judged by our race or gender, our mental capacity, physical shape, or stamina? Are people to be ranked by how they look, or what they know, or what they can do? Is our own sense of worth and our treatment of other people dependent upon biological characteristics? Is the meaning of life to be found in satisfying biological needs and appetites? Is there any existence beyond biological death and decay?

In addition to their biological qualities, human beings have always been tempted to define themselves by political affiliations and to root their identity in nations, ethnicity, social classes, religious affiliations, and ideologies. Defining one's essence by national origin has been a favorite idolatry since human beings first formed themselves into political entities. Being American, German, French, Italian, Korean, Zimbabwean, Peruvian, Egyptian, or Israeli can easily become more important than being a child of God. When the nation's ethnicity or ideology becomes primary in determining our self-concept or our treatment of others, the primary source of human identity is denied. Our common kinship with God and other people is sacrificed to other gods. Distinctions between people become sources of conflict, competition, and coercion rather than gifts to be woven into the fabric of our common humanity and celebrated as signs of God's grace.

The Book of Jonah is an early judgment upon the assumption of national and religious superiority and the separation of peoples into "friends" and "enemies." Jonah assumed the superiority of his

nation over his despised enemies, the people of Nineveh. He wanted
their destruction. He was repulsed by the notion that God would have
mercy on the Ninevites. Jonah learned, however, that his enemies were
not God's enemies. God's mercy and compassion included those from
whom Jonah sought to distance himself.

The Market Logic of Exchange

A major threat to our identity as persons made in the divine image is
economics and the market logic of exchange.[5] As we stated in chapter
two, the market with its consumerism has become a prevailing god in
the contemporary world. In a consumerist culture, persons are valued
and measured by what they can produce and exchange in the marketplace. Although exchange is an important, necessary component of our
economic life, the logic of exchange has slipped into the human psyche
as a means of defining the nature or purpose of human beings. The
logic of exchange reduces people to commodities and relationships to
utilitarian transactions.

An illustration of the devastating consequences of evaluating
human beings based on exchange value is the comment of an eighty-
year-old man. He is in declining health and unable to work. The aging
process is diminishing his energy and he now relies on his family to do
many things he once did. Confronting his growing physical limitations
and increased dependency, he said with regret and almost despair, "I'm
not worth anything. I'm no good to anyone now."

A society that defines people in terms of what they have of value
to exchange eventually leaves its members demoralized, depleted, and
"useless." Highly prized, marketable traits or qualities—such as youth-
ful appearance, sex appeal, physical stamina, mental acumen, and
productivity—eventually wane for everyone. As they diminish, so do
self-esteem, hope, joy, and meaningful relationships. Since such values
are subject to forces beyond our control, people who root their worth
in them are always insecure.

The image of God in human beings is rooted in grace—God's
unmerited, undeserved love. Our status as children of God is nothing
we have or could earn. It is a gift bestowed, not an achievement reached.

Self-identity and relationships, therefore, operate by the logic of grace rather than the logic of exchange and merit. Since being made in the divine image is a status God bestows and makes possible through the power of the Holy Spirit, our identity and worth are not contingent upon precarious things such as appearance, mental and physical stamina, productivity, or economic security.

But what does it mean to be made in the image of God?

Made in God's Image

The *imago Dei* has been interpreted in differing ways in the history of the church. Some interpretations have been destructive to humanity. They have resulted in the distortion of the divine image. For example, it has been contended that the divine image has to do primarily with dominion over the rest of creation. A consequence of such an interpretation has been the exploitation of creation by human beings. Or, some have used "made in God's image" as a statement about gender, implying male superiority and dominance. Both distortions pervert the meaning of the doctrine and provide a theological rationale for behavior and relationships that are contrary to the nature of God.

John Wesley saw *imago Dei*—image of God—in three manifestations:

1. The natural image, in which the human capacity for understanding, freedom of the will, and love are expressions of God's image;
2. The political image, in which human beings exercise stewardship over creation and share in God's ongoing governance of the earth; and
3. The moral image, in which the human potential for righteousness, true holiness, and happiness are signs of the divine image.[6]

For Wesley, the image of God denotes the human capacity for knowing and responding to God's grace, which is God's presence and power to heal, forgive, reconcile, and transform. He proclaimed: "It was free grace that 'formed man of the dust of the ground, and breathed into him a living soul,' and stamped on that soul the image of God."[7]

Being created in God's image has to do primarily with relationship rather than with inherent qualities within human beings. God has created and called human beings to live in covenant fidelity with God the Father, the Son, and the Holy Spirit. As the triune God is defined by oneness in the diversity of the relationship between the Father, Jesus Christ, and the Holy Spirit, human beings are relational creatures whose basic identity is known only in relationship with the triune God. Our origin is in God who claims and calls us. Our destiny is in being conformed to the image of Jesus Christ by the power of the Holy Spirit.

Origin, Calling, Identity, and Destiny

The image of God is a declaration of the depth of our relationship with and dependence upon God. By the power of the Holy Spirit we are incorporated into the life and destiny of Jesus Christ, who is "the image of the invisible God" (Colossians 1:15). Human beings are creatures created and claimed by God, called to conform to the likeness of Jesus Christ (2 Corinthians 3:18), and whose bodies are "a temple of the Holy Spirit" (1 Corinthians 6:19). Being made in the image of God means: We are created by God with the capacity to know and love God and one another; we have been incorporated into the life and destiny of Jesus Christ; and the Holy Spirit dwells within us as One who is ever working to conform us to the likeness of Christ, who is the true image of God. The vocation of every human being is to be "in such relationship to the origin, the provision, and the end of all creation that God appears through us."[8]

The writer of the First Epistle of John summarized the identity, calling, and destiny of human beings in these words:

> See what love the Father has given us, that we should be called children of God; and that is what we are. The reason the world does not know us is that it did not know him. Beloved, we are God's children now; what we will be has not yet been revealed. What we do know is this: when he is revealed, we will be like him, for we will see him as he is. (3:1-2)

As creatures in the divine image, our origin, calling, identity, and destiny are in Christ who is the image of God. Our identity and destiny lie in this affirmation: We belong to God!

Conclusion

In many ways, human identity is formed by relationships. We take on the values, qualities, dreams, and goals of those to whom we relate in significant and ongoing ways. Critical to the health and wholeness of persons is a loving relationship with parents, those who gave us life. Parents give us our genetic traits that form much of our identity and destiny. They birth us into a family with a story and a constellation of relationships. We are shaped by relationships other than with parents— brothers and sisters, friends and colleagues, spouses and children. Out of these relationships emerge our own identity and destiny.

There is a relationship that goes before, permeates, and transcends our relationships with family, friends, and colleagues. It is the primal relationship that shapes and molds all others. It is our relationship with the Triune God. Our origin is in God who created humanity in the divine image; called human beings to a common vocation of being the reflection of God's likeness; incorporated human beings into the life and destiny of Jesus Christ; and empowers us by the power of the Holy Spirit to conform to the One who is "the image of the invisible God, the firstborn of all creation" (Colossians 1:15). Wesley affirmed this relationship in these words:

> How truly wise is this man! . . . He knows God: his Father and his friend, parent of all good, the center of the spirits of all flesh, the sole happiness of all intelligent beings. He sees, clearer than the light of the noonday sun, that this is the end of human life: to glorify God who made us for himself, and to love and enjoy God for ever. And with equal clearness he sees the means to that end, to the enjoyment of God in glory; even now to know, to love, to imitate God, and to believe in Jesus Christ whom God hath sent.[9]

Our identity as creatures made in God's image is denied by much in the contemporary world and in our own experience. Other sources of defining who we are seem more compelling and self-evident. We are bombarded with messages that we are our biological needs, drives, and characteristics; therefore, fulfillment comes from satisfying our biological impulses and preserving and/or enhancing our biological assets. The temptation to root our identity and destiny in our national and ethnic origins or our ideological or religious affiliations is pervasive and persuasive. Being an American or a United Methodist becomes more important than celebrating and living our identity as children of God. The exchange logic of consumerism promises self-fulfillment in having, accumulating, consuming. Everything, including relationships and even God, becomes a commodity to be used to fulfill our self-defined goals.

Although made in God's image, human beings have accepted other identities and destinies. The result is the distortion of true humanity and the refusal of God's invitation to share in God's own life and mission in the world. Made with the capacity for living in covenantal fidelity with God, humanity has turned toward relationships with gods other than the Creator. The divine image is distorted. Made "a little lower than God, and crowned . . . with glory and honor" (Psalm 8:5), human beings have settled for far less than their God-given identity and Christ-won destiny. Such is the essence of sin!

Opportunities for Reflection

The following questions may be used by groups wishing to discuss the material in chapter four or by individuals wanting to reflect on issues raised within the chapter.

1. How do you define yourself? What role do such things as jobs, titles, physical characteristics, educational degrees, and accomplishments play in your own identity and self-esteem?

2. If human beings are made in the image of God, how do we respond to stories of the exploitation of children in sweatshops, prostitution and sex trafficking, the widespread popularity of pornography, and the labeling of people as "enemies," "terrorists," or "criminals"? What are the implications of the *imago Dei* on such issues as pornography, abortion, capital punishment, and war?

3. When do you feel most worthless and insignificant? What accounts for such feelings? When do you feel most valued and significant?

4. How do we help others to know their identity as persons created in the image of God?

5

The Divine Image Distorted

Humans are created to share communion with the Triune God. Every person's primary vocation or calling is the fulfilling of his/her identity as a beloved child of God made in the image of God. Having been created and redeemed as children of God, we are to live in such relationship with our Creator, Redeemer, and Sustainer so that God is made known in the world. The God who gives us such a lofty identity and destiny also shows us in Jesus Christ the perfect image of the divine. God does even more! Through the presence and power of the Holy Spirit, we are made part of the life and destiny of Jesus Christ and conformed to his likeness.

Something, however, has gone tragically wrong. Created to live in covenantal fidelity with the Triune God, human beings have betrayed the covenant, broken the relationship, and followed other gods. Made to live in freedom, we are enslaved by addictions and habits that distort the image of the God of liberation. Endued with the capacity to love as Jesus loves, we are caught in a web of selfishness, violence, and exploitation that threatens human existence. Called to share in God's care and nurture of creation, humans plunder and poison the earth's resources, threatening its survival. Invited to share in the divine creativity by using gifts bestowed upon us by the Holy Spirit, we delight in defacing and degrading life's beauty and goodness. Promised "You shall be holy, for I the Lord your God am holy" (Leviticus 19:2), humanity defames and distorts God's nature, eschewing holiness of heart and life.

Our own experiences and observations provide ample evidence that more than God's image is at work in humanity. Gods other than the One known as Father, Son, and Holy Spirit shape and mold our lives. The Apostle Paul described the human condition in these words:

> For you did not receive a spirit of slavery to fall back into fear, but you have received a spirit of adoption . . . For the creation waits with eager longing for the revealing of the children of God . . . that the creation itself will be set free from its bondage to decay and will obtain the freedom of the glory of the children of God. We know that the whole creation has been groaning in labor pains until now; and not only the creation, but we ourselves, who have the first fruits of the Spirit, groan inwardly while we wait for adoption, the redemption of our bodies. (Romans 8:15, 19, 21-22)

Our United Methodist doctrinal standards declare that sin is "the corruption of the nature of every man [human], that naturally is engendered of the offspring of Adam, whereby man [humanity] is very far gone from original righteousness, and of his own nature inclined to evil, and that continually."[1] The standards for doctrine also state, "We believe man [humanity] is fallen from righteousness and, apart from the grace of our Lord Jesus Christ, is destitute of holiness and inclined to evil."[2]

Sin Is Real

The divine image in humanity is distorted by sin. John Wesley believed that every manifestation of God's image in human beings has been stained and perverted. The "natural image" with its capacity for understanding, freedom, and love has been permeated by confusion, bondage, and hatred. We are blind to the purposes and presence of God, captive to our own appetites and desires, and filled with selfishness, apathy, and animosity. The political image, which gives us the ability to share in God's care and nurture of the world, is distorted by greed and exploitation. Our potential for righteousness and holiness—the moral image—is twisted and defamed by pervasive evil that invades our thoughts, relationships, and actions.[3]

In his sermon entitled "The One Thing Needful," Wesley describes the condition of humanity:

> But sin hath now effaced the image of God. He [humanity] is no longer nearly allied to angels. He is sunk lower than the very beasts of the field. His soul is not only earthly and sensual, but devilish. Thus is the mighty fallen! The glory is departed from him! His brightness is swallowed up in utter darkness!
>
> From the glorious liberty wherein he was made he is fallen into the basest bondage. The devil, whose slave he now is, to work his will, hath him so fast in prison that he cannot get forth. He hath bound him with a thousand chains, the heavy chains of his own vile affections. For every inordinate appetite, every unholy passion, as it is the express image of the god of this world, so it is the most galling yoke, the most grievous chain, that can bind a free-born spirit. And with these is every child of Adam, everyone that is born into this world, so loaded that he cannot lift up an eye, a thought to heaven; that his whole soul cleaveth unto the dust![4]

Every part of humanity has been infected with sin. Human identity has been distorted. "Our body, soul, and spirit, are infected, overspread, consumed, with the most fatal leprosy. We are all over, within and without, in the eye of God, full of diseases, and wounds, and putrifying sores."[5]

Various explanations of the nature and origin of sin have been offered by theologians. Reinhold Niebuhr's account of sin as pride is well known. Sin is succumbing to the inevitable temptation to compete with God for dominance and control. It is thinking that we are gods rather than daughters and sons of God. But sin is also sloth, which makes us less than children of God. It is the failure to be the image of God in which we have been created. Sin is falling short of our true identity and our refusal of kinship with the One in whose likeness we are made.

Sin is more than behavior or personal habits that can be changed with effort or simple remedy. Sin has to do with "missing the mark," failing to be who God invites us to be. It is reflecting other than the "image of God." It is a disease of the soul for which human beings cannot cure themselves. It disfigures, distorts, and thwarts God's intention for humanity.

Wesley rooted sin in the liberty that God bestowed upon human beings. He defined sin as a willful, voluntary transgression of the known will of God. Human beings have chosen to use their freedom in ways that deny kinship. Rather than accepting the invitation to share in God's life and mission, we declare independence from God and live in competition with and rebellion against the Creator.

SIN'S PERVASIVE POWER

Sin is personal, individual, corporate, and systemic. It is lodged within the human heart and within the structures and practices of cultures, nations, and institutions. We are born into a web of such systemic distortions of God's intention for humanity as racism, sexism, and economic and political injustice; and before we are conscious of it, we are captive to societal values and forces outside our control.

The doctrine of original sin affirms that sin is inescapable, pervasive, and systemic. The Articles of Religion of The Methodist Church states: "Original sin standeth not in the following of Adam (as the Pelagians do vainly talk), but it is the corruption of the nature of every man [human being] . . ."[6] Original sin further describes evil's power over humanity: "The condition of man [humanity] after the fall of Adam is such that he cannot turn and prepare himself, by his own natural strength and works, to faith . . ."[7]

The doctrine of original sin means that sin has deeper roots than individual or personal choices. Sin is so pervasive in human personality and in society that we cannot avoid captivity to it. Before we are conscious of having a choice, we have already become victims of sin. For example, we inevitably assume the values of the prevailing culture. People born into a society that views African-Americans as inferior become prejudiced without initially choosing to do so. Or, a male who grows up in an environment that assigns a subordinate role to women is likely to be sexist without realizing it. This disease of the soul—sin— infects all human beings. It invades every aspect of life and is built into structures, policies, and practices of institutions and nations. No areas of human existence are left untouched by sin's presence. Even our best remains tainted and fails to fulfill the divine image.

The power of sin exceeds human strength. It is more than a personal inclination or temptation that can be defeated by willpower. As the Apostle Paul wrote, "For our struggle is not against enemies of blood and flesh, but against the rulers, against the authorities, against the cosmic powers of this present darkness, against the spiritual forces of evil in the heavenly places" (Ephesians 6:12). Demonic forces pervade institutions, individuals, cultures, and systems. They create injustice, oppression, and cruelty, and we fall victim to their prey without realizing it. The insidious powers of sin and death assault humanity with weapons of deceit, treachery, coercion, manipulation, and violence. The results are the persistent distortion of the divine image in humanity, the breaking of covenant with God, and a creation threatened with destruction.

RELUCTANCE TO ACKNOWLEDGE SIN

An adult Sunday school class in a United Methodist Church requested a session with the pastor. The class of young adults objected to the use of prayers of confession in the Sunday morning worship service. The reasons given for their objections were these:

- We are not guilty of some of the sins identified.
- The prayers either imply or state that "we are unworthy of God's love."
- Confession is negative and worship should promote positive feelings.
- Calling people sinners damages their self-image.

When asked how they would account for the apparent evil in themselves and the world, members of the class talked in terms of "emotional problems," "psychological needs," "sickness," and "maladjustment." Therapy, personal discipline, and support groups were seen as more appropriate remedies for human imperfections than repentance and confession of sin.

The church's understanding of sin seems archaic to modern ears, even to the people called Methodists! Other explanations seem more sophisticated and plausible. Referring to men and women as sinners and calling harmful and hurtful behavior "sin" is considered to be insensitive, judgmental, and harsh. Understanding human beings as sinners is thought by some to cause psychological damage by preventing a positive self-esteem.

True, people can be damaged by an emphasis on sin. The misuse of the doctrine contributes to further distortion of the image of God in humanity. It can be interpreted in a way that justifies self-hate, judgmental behavior, cruelty, and emotional sickness. Many people bear the scars of a "hellfire and damnation" religion that describes people as worthless sinners awaiting the eternal damnation and punishment of a wrathful God. The doctrine of original sin has also been used to justify negative attitudes toward sexuality and women.

The misuse of the doctrine of sin, however, does not warrant its removal from our vocabulary and understanding. Wesley confronted considerable resistance to his own preaching about sin. The emerging "age of reason" of the eighteenth century went to considerable lengths to counter the church's traditional arguments about human "depravity." The following excerpt from Wesley's sermon, "Original Sin," sounds as if it could have been written today. He began the sermon by acknowledging that teachers and preachers throughout history have provided glowing descriptions "concerning the nature of man [humanity], as if it were all innocence and perfection." He added:

> Accounts of this kind have particularly abounded in the present century; and perhaps in no part of the world more than in our own country. Here not a few persons of strong understanding, as well as extensive learning, have employed their utmost abilities to show what they termed "the fair side of human nature." And it must be acknowledged that if their accounts of him be just, man is still but "a little lower than the angels . . ."[8]

Wesley admitted that positive accounts of human nature are widely read and believed. He laments, "So that it is now quite unfashionable to talk otherwise, to say anything to the disparagement of human nature; which is generally allowed, notwithstanding a few infirmities, to be very innocent and wise and virtuous."[9] The notion of the innate goodness of human beings has a long history. But to ignore the reality of human sinfulness, according to United Methodist doctrine, is to deny the Bible and human experience and to perpetuate human captivity to sin.

WHATEVER BECAME OF SIN?

The eminent psychiatrist, Karl Menninger, wrote a book in 1973 entitled, *Whatever Became of Sin?* Based on his experience in dealing with human emotions and behavior, Dr. Menninger called for a recovery of the doctrine of sin. He warned against designating all negative behavior and destructive traits in human beings as sickness or maladjustment. According to the psychiatrist, assuming that psychotherapy and medicine can cure every human ailment ignores and leaves untreated humankind's most serious problem—sin.[10]

In the early 1990s, the *New York Times* carried a reprint of a *Wall Street Journal* editorial. The provocative editorial was followed by this tag line: "When was the last time you had a good conversation about sin?" The editorial referred to a number of the moral dilemmas appearing daily in the media. There followed this comment:

> Sin isn't something that many people, including most churches, have spent much time talking about or worrying about through the years of the (cultural and sexual) revolution. But we will say this for sin; it at least offered a frame of reference for personal behavior. When the frame was dismantled, guilt wasn't the only thing that fell away; we also lost the guidewire of personal responsibility. . . . Everyone was left on his or her own. It now appears that many wrecked people could have used a road map.[11]

SIN HAS CONSEQUENCES

Wesley was correct in saying that the sinfulness of humanity can be denied only by ignoring the Bible and experience. Certainly, scripture affirms the pervasiveness, power, and destructiveness of sin. From

Genesis to Revelation, the drama of evil's power and humanity's refusal to share obediently and lovingly in God's own life and mission unfolds. The Bible is the story of human flight from the One in whom humanity finds its home. From Adam and Eve's hiding in guilt and shame, to Cain's murder of his brother, to the crucifixion of Jesus Christ, the distortion of the image of God in humanity appears as a constant theme in the biblical story. The New Testament declares, "all have sinned and fall short of the glory of God" (Romans 3:23), and "If we say we have no sin, we deceive ourselves, and the truth is not in us" (1 John 1:8).

The tragic consequences of such distortion are revealed graphically in the cross. The crucifixion is more than the execution of an innocent man; it is a dramatization of sin's power and consequences and God's response. Systemic and personal sinfulness results in needless suffering and catastrophic destruction. As the New Testament warns, "the wages of sin is death" (Romans 6:23). The consequence of persistent denial and betrayal of the divine image is suffering—the suffering of God. God so closely identifies with the human family that God assumes the suffering and death inflicted upon it. The cross of Christ, then, represents sin's tragic consequences upon humanity and upon God.

DAILY AWARENESS OF SIN

We are daily confronted with the consequences of sin. The media bring scenes of needless suffering into our homes: children dying from hunger and neglect caused by economic injustice, young men and women killed and wounded in war and violence, elderly persons suffering from loneliness, people caged in prisons and jails, the earth itself being poisoned and depleted, men and women addicted to drugs and alcohol, the homeless wandering the world's streets..

The distortion of the divine image has consequences more personal than scenes on television screens. Our own inner lives and our relationships bear the scars of a distorted identity. An incessant anxiety stalks us. Feelings of inadequacy and fear of being unable to measure up drive us to compulsive competition and conspicuous consumption. Dread of growing old and dying robs us of hope and joy. Betrayal and neglect of covenants with spouses and children leave us ashamed and guilty. Tensions, mistrust, alienation, and anger plague our relationships.

Loneliness and meaninglessness invade us and defeat the optimism and mission that once pulled us toward the future. We often feel lost in a dangerous wilderness, away from home. The words of Charles Wesley capture our longings to be free from the distortion of our true identity:

Depth of mercy!
Can there be mercy still reserved for me?
Can my God his wrath forbear, me,
the chief of sinners, spare?

I have long withstood his grace,
long provoked him to his face,
would not hearken to his calls,
grieved him by a thousand falls.

I my Master have denied,
I afresh have crucified,
oft profaned his hallowed name,
put him to an open shame.

There for me the Savior stands,
Shows his wounds and spreads his hands.
God is love! I know, I feel;
Jesus weeps and loves me still.

Now incline me to repent,
let me now my sins lament,
now my foul revolt deplore,
weep, believe, and sin no more.[12]

Conclusion

The divine image in which human beings are made has been distorted and disfigured, causing enormous suffering and anguish to both humans and God. The failure to live in the image of God and share God's life and mission is the essence and origin of sin. Sin is universal, pervasive, and inescapable. Its power permeates every aspect of life and thwarts God's intention for all creation. The cross of Jesus Christ represents the tragic consequences of sin. Sin seeks the death and destruction of the image and purpose of God, who enters into the suffering and death of humanity.

But sin is not the last word! It is not the most powerful and pervasive reality in the universe! What humanity cannot do—restore the divine image—God does. The One who created us in God's image and invited us into covenantal relationship takes the initiative to restore the image. In Jesus Christ, God enters the wilderness to set humanity free and to lead the prodigal sons and daughters home. God, in Christ, takes on the principalities and powers and triumphs over them!

John Wesley considered the restoration of the divine image to be the heart of authentic religion. He proclaimed: "Ye know that the great end of religion is to renew our hearts in the image of God, to repair that total loss of righteousness and true holiness which we sustained by the sin of our first parent."[13]

Where is God? The "crucified" God is wherever there is suffering and sin!

What is God doing? Through the power of the Holy Spirit and the redemptive life, death, and resurrection of Jesus, God is working to restore the divine image in humanity, bringing creation itself into conformity with Jesus Christ—the image of the invisible God. What is the appropriate response to this God? Accept the grace of God, which goes before us, saves us, and transforms us.

Opportunities for Reflection

The following questions may be used by groups wishing to discuss the material in chapter five or by individuals wanting to reflect on issues raised within the chapter.

1. In what ways does sin disfigure, distort, or thwart God's intention for your life? For your congregation? For the world?
2. In what ways can people be damaged by an emphasis on sin?
3. In what ways are you confronted with the consequences of sin?
4. What role, if any, does a prayer of confession play in the worship services in your church? Should such a prayer be part of each Sunday service? Why? Why not?

6

Reconciled and Transformed by Grace

The United Methodist doctrinal/theological statement declares: "The created order is designed for the well-being of all creatures and as the place of human dwelling in covenant with God. As sinful creatures, however, we have broken that covenant, become estranged from God, wounded ourselves and one another, and wreaked havoc throughout the natural order. We stand in need of redemption."[1]

The essence and purpose of "real religion," says John Wesley, is "a restoration of [man] by Him that bruises the serpent's head to all that the old serpent deprived him of; a restoration not only to the favour but the likeness to the image of God . . . Nothing short of this is the Christian religion."[2] Wesley's principal concern was "the order of salvation." Albert Outler, one of the foremost Wesleyan scholars, wrote, "The controlling theological inquiry throughout his life was into the meaning of becoming and being a Christian in all the aspects of Christian existence."[3] Methodism is rooted in the belief that God seeks to reconcile the whole creation and restore all persons into the image of Jesus Christ. In spite of humanity's distortion of the divine image and the betrayal of covenantal fidelity, God the Creator is for us in Jesus Christ and with us in the Holy Spirit, and is always before us, bringing into being a new creation.

The Methodist movement considered sharing in God's reconciling and transforming action to be its mission. Both in England and in America, early Methodists believed that God had raised them "to reform the nation, particularly the Church, and to spread Scriptural holiness over the land."[4] Nothing short of participating in God's initiative to reclaim humanity and reform the whole of creation has formed the foundation of Methodism's existence.

Central to Methodism is the emphasis upon grace as the source of salvation, the restoration of the divine image and the reconciliation of creation. "Grace pervades our understanding of Christian faith and life," affirms *The Book of Discipline*.[5] Although we share with other Christians a belief in salvation by grace, Methodist traditions have combined the manifestations of grace in a manner to create distinctive emphases for living the full Christian life. A recovery of those emphases can be a means by which we are reconciled to God and renewed in the image of God.

Grace: God's Presence and Power

The Book of Discipline defines grace as "the undeserved, unmerited, and loving action of God in human existence through the ever-present Holy Spirit."[6] It affirms that "God's grace is manifest in all creation even though suffering, violence, and evil are everywhere present."[7] Rather than grace being a packaged gift dispensed by God, grace is God's presence and power to create, heal, forgive, reconcile, and transform persons, communities, nations, and the entire cosmos. Where God is present there is grace, God's power to renew and transform.

Wesley defined grace as God's "bounty, or favour: his free, undeserved favour, . . . man having no claim to the least of his mercies. It was free grace that 'formed man of the dust of the ground, and breathed into him a living soul,' and stamped on that soul the image of God, and 'put all things under his feet.' . . . For there is nothing we are, or have, or do, which can deserve the least thing at God's hand."[8]

According to Randy Maddox, Wesley was deeply concerned to hold together the two traditional emphases on grace.[9] The Eastern Church has historically placed the accent on grace as God's healing, while the Western Church has emphasized pardon as the principal work of grace. John Wesley incorporated both healing and pardon as inseparable expressions of divine grace. In a letter to Alexander Knox in 1778, he wrote: "It will be a double blessing if you give yourself up to the Great Physician, that He may heal soul and body together. And unquestionably this is His design. He wants to give you . . . both inward and outward health."[10] The total integration of personality and relationships is the ongoing work of divine grace.

Grace is God doing on our behalf what we could never do for ourselves—create ourselves in the image of God, reconcile ourselves to God whose life we have denied and distorted, restore the divine image in humanity, and transform ourselves and creation into the likeness of Jesus Christ. Grace is Jesus Christ! It is God's response to Paul's cry of despair, "Wretched man that I am! Who will rescue me from this body of death? Thanks be to God through Jesus Christ our Lord!" (Romans 7:24-25). Grace is God: "God, who is rich in mercy, out of the great love with which he loved us even when we were dead through our trespasses, made us alive together with Christ—by grace you have been saved . . ." (Ephesians 2:4-5).

God's grace is universal and available to all persons. The divine presence and power permeate all of life with potential for beauty, goodness, truth, and love. Grace is God's gifts bestowed, God's gifts received, God's gifts shared, and God's gifts transformed. Living in accordance with grace orients life around God's gift of salvation. We trust that God is before us, for us, and with us in the journey toward the fulfillment of our identity and destiny.

Although grace is one as the Triune God is One, grace in the Methodist tradition is understood as manifested in three actions:

- Prevenient Grace
- Justifying (saving) Grace
- Sanctifying Grace

Every stage on the journey toward salvation is made possible by God's grace.

PREVENIENT GRACE—GRACE THAT PREPARES US

Although Methodists recognize the seriousness of sin and the tragic distortion of God's image in humanity, we believe that God's grace prevents the total destruction of the divine image in us. However distorted our identity as beloved sons or daughters of God, grace prevents the complete obliteration of that identity and ever works to prod, woo, and prepare us for redemption and renewal. Therefore, no one is beyond redemption!

Prevenient grace is defined in *The Book of Discipline* as "the divine love that surrounds all humanity and precedes any and all of our conscious impulses. This grace prompts our first wish to please God, our first glimmer of understanding concerning God's will, and our 'first slight transient conviction' of having sinned against God."[11] Prevenient grace is our way of declaring that God always goes before us and any action on our part is preceded by God's action, preparing us for wholeness and healing.

Prevenient grace means that God's presence and power reside throughout all creation—the natural order, in the human conscience, in the relationships into which we are born. The love of family, the Christian community, the sacraments, the pangs of guilt, the longings for meaning and purpose and love, and the awareness of our alienation are all expressions of prevenient grace. They are the essence of prevenient grace.

The assurance that grace always precedes our response and actions enabled early Methodists to proclaim the gospel boldly and confidently to people marginalized by the world, such as the impoverished and the imprisoned. The Methodist preachers trusted that God was already present in the mines and slums, in the prisons and on the gallows, awakening persons to their identity as children of God and preparing them for conversion. A "desire to flee from the wrath to come"[12] was the only requirement for membership in the Methodist Societies. That is, Methodism was open to those in whom prevenient grace was prompting, convicting, and drawing them toward the restoration of their true identity.

Prevenient grace is the "prodigal son" in Luke's Gospel becoming aware of his lost identity:

> But when he came to himself he said, "How many of my father's hired hands have bread enough and to spare, but here I am dying of hunger! I will get up and go to my father, and I will say to him, 'Father, I have sinned against heaven and before you; I am no longer worthy to be called your son . . .'" (Luke 15:17-19)

Longing for home, awareness of betrayal, prompting to repent— these are manifestations of grace preparing us for a new future.

Wesley described prevenient grace as the porch of religion. It is the place where we prepare to enter the house. It is possible to live one's life on the porch, the very edges of home, with only glimpses of and longings for fellowship with the family. But God does not leave us on the porch, on the edges of home. As we live on the porch, we not only long to be in the house, but we feel unworthy of entering. God's grace, however, enables us to enter our true home and claim our place in the family.

JUSTIFYING GRACE—GRACE FOR US

The door into the house of God's salvation is justification, or *justifying grace*. "Justification," said Wesley, "is another word for pardon. It is the forgiveness of all our sins, and . . . our acceptance with God."[13] Justifying grace is the assurance of forgiveness that comes from repentance, from turning toward God's gracious gift of life in Jesus Christ. It is being made right with God, being reconciled through Christ to the Creator whose covenant we have betrayed and whose image we have distorted. *The Book of Discipline* affirms: "In justification we are, through faith, forgiven our sin and restored to God's favor. This righting of relationships by God through Christ calls forth our faith and trust as we experience regeneration, by which we are made new creatures in Christ."[14]

As prevenient grace is something God does before us, justifying grace is that which God does for us in Jesus Christ. We are adopted into the life, death, and resurrection of Jesus Christ who intercedes for us. What we cannot do—atone for our sins—Christ does for us. Justifying grace is God in Christ affirming that we are still daughters and sons of God. Faith is turning away from an identity shaped by idols and turning toward our kinship with God. It is taking personally what God has done for all humankind in Jesus Christ.

Wesley's description of his experience at Aldersgate Street is an example of justifying grace. After years of attempting to be reconciled to God by strict obedience and failing as a missionary in America, Wesley joined a small group of Christians who gathered at Aldersgate Street for Bible study and prayer. He wrote of the experience:

> About a quarter before nine, while he [the leader] was describing the change which God works in the heart through faith in Christ, I felt my heart strangely warmed. I felt I did trust in Christ, Christ alone for salvation, and an assurance was given me that he had taken away my sins, even mine, and saved me from the law of sin and death.[15]

Wesley insisted that faith in Christ is the sole necessary and sufficient cause of justification. Faith is trusting Christ's death as "for me." It is acting upon what God has done in Jesus Christ as the basis of our status with God. Faith, trust in Christ, is also a gift from God and not a human achievement. Assurance of pardon and our status as restored children of God are not dependent upon feelings. For Wesley, the assurance of justification was evidenced in the changed lives of those to whom God's justifying grace was proclaimed.

The process of justification and new birth as restored children of God is often referred to as conversion, which is the appropriation of justifying grace. It is a change in how we view ourselves, others, and the world around us. Our doctrinal/theological statement recognizes that "Such a change may be sudden and dramatic, or gradual and cumulative. It marks a new beginning, yet it is part of an ongoing process."[16]

Another term used to describe justification is "new birth" or being "born again." Just as physical birth is a complex process with interrelated experiences, the new birth also includes multiple components. No two births are identical. Spiritual birth begins with conception (God's secret) and continues in gestation (justification). Then comes birth (justification), followed by growth (sanctification) and maturity (Christian perfection). Each experience is inseparable from the others. All are shrouded in mystery and transcendence.

Justification is more than the forgiveness of our individual sin and the restoring of our personal relationship with God. It is incorporation into community. Through justifying grace, we are incorporated into Christ's community in which people are accepted and affirmed as children of God. We become members of a new family in which kinship transcends genetics, geography, and even religion. It is a community built upon and shaped by the person of Jesus Christ and the power of the Holy Spirit, not merit or earthly status. By accepting and affirming our God-given identity and destiny as children of God, we affirm our solidarity with all whom God loves and for whom Christ died.

Realization that our worth, identity, kinship, and destiny are rooted in the God who is before us and for us is the essence of justifying grace. To accept that status and enter the doorway of a new creation is the beginning of our salvation. It is an identity—a destiny that we can never earn, nor can it be taken from us. God, however, does more with sin than forgive it. God's grace goes beyond giving us status as sons and daughters of God.

SANCTIFYING GRACE—GRACE PERFECTING US

God's goal for humanity is the complete restoration of the divine image and the total conformity of all creation to the image of Jesus Christ. Sanctification (from *sanctus*, meaning "holy") denotes the process by which the believer is made holy following justification.

The Book of Discipline states, "We hold that the wonder of God's acceptance and pardon does not end God's saving work, which continues to nurture our growth in grace. Through the power of the Holy Spirit we are enabled to increase in the knowledge and love of God and in love for our neighbor."[17] If prevenient grace is the porch of the house of grace and justifying grace is the doorway, *sanctifying grace* represents the rooms in the infinite dwelling of God's presence.

Wesley referred to sanctification as the grand depositum of Methodism. For Wesley, justification is what God does *for* us—the forgiveness of sins and incorporation into a new community; sanctification is what God does *in* us—holiness of life, the entire love of God shed abroad in our hearts. Justification launches the process of being conformed to the image of Christ. Through the power of the Holy

Spirit, God creates in the believer "holiness of heart and life." Grace is not content to give us a new status before God; it creates in us a *new being* characterized by holiness.

The doctrine of Christian perfection represents a distinctive emphasis of historic Methodism. Methodist preachers have been asked since the days of Wesley: Have you faith in Christ? Are you going on to perfection? Do you expect to be made perfect in love in this life? Are you earnestly striving after it? These historic questions assume an understanding of "Christian perfection" or holiness of heart and life. They are not so much affirmations of human potential as they are affirmations of the power of God's grace in Jesus Christ to make us new creatures.

Sanctifying grace draws us toward the gift of Christian perfection, which Wesley described as a heart "habitually filled with the love of God and neighbor" and "having the mind of Christ and walking as he walked."[18] Sanctification is the process of maturing in discipleship until the heart is habitually inclined to do what is right. Perfection—sanctification or holiness—is not to be equated with perfectionism or flawlessness. Neither is it an achievement; it is a gift emerging from friendship with and obedience to Christ. One may never attain the state of sinlessness. Wesley, however, was convinced that it is possible to so love God that one loses the desire to sin and consistently lives in the light of God's love.

Love is the definition of perfection. Wesley wrote, "Pure love reigning alone in the heart and life, this is the whole of scripture perfection."[19] The commandment in the Sermon on the Mount, "Be perfect, therefore, as your heavenly Father is perfect" (Matthew 5:48), is in the context of Jesus' teaching regarding love as including even our enemies. All commandments are summed up in one: "You shall love the Lord your God with all your heart, and with all your soul, and with all your mind" (Matthew 22:37); and "You shall love your neighbor as yourself" (Matthew 22:39). Wesley understood the commands of Christ as "covered commands." What Christ *commands*, Christ *covers* with the grace that enables us to fulfill them. In other words, Christ does not command us to do what Christ does not empower us to do.

Perhaps the height and breadth of sanctifying grace is best expressed in verses from Charles Wesley's beloved hymn "Love Divine, All Loves Excelling":

Love divine, all loves excelling,
joy of heaven to earth come down;
    fix in us thy humble dwelling;
    all thy faithful mercies crown!
Jesus, thou art all compassion,
pure, unbounded love thou art;
    visit us with thy salvation;
    enter every trembling heart.

Breathe, O breathe thy loving Spirit
    into every troubled breast!
Let us all in thee inherent;
    let us find that second rest.
Take away our bent to sinning;
Alpha and Omega be;
    end of faith, as its beginning,
    set our hearts at liberty.

Finish, then, thy new creation;
    pure and spotless let us be.
Let us see thy great salvation
Perfectly restored in thee;
changed from glory into glory,
    till in heaven we take our place,
    till we cast our crowns before thee,
    lost in wonder, love, and praise.[20]

GLORIFYING GRACE—PERSONAL AND SOCIAL TRANSFORMATION

John Wesley affirmed, "The gospel of Christ knows of no religion, but social; no holiness but social holiness."[21] His immediate concern, in this specific context, was to stress that we cannot be Christian in isolation. Growth in love for God and neighbor requires practices within a community devoted to sharing in God's life and mission. But it is also clear that Wesley was convinced that God's grace does not stop with the healing and pardon of individuals; God's presence and power is directed toward the transformation of the entire creation, from human hearts to wayward stars.

The theme of Jesus' preaching and the broader framework of the Methodist movement was the kingdom of God. God is bringing a new world of justice, righteousness, generosity, and joy. Nothing less than a new heaven and a new earth conformed to Jesus Christ is God's vision for creation. The victory that God won in Jesus Christ will be consummated and, wherever God's righteousness exists, the kingdom is already present.

Methodists have understood that the kingdom of God, announced and inaugurated by Jesus Christ, has tangible social consequences in society. The kingdom is both inward in the heart of the believer and outward in the life of the world. The kingdom is both a present reality and a future hope. It is present wherever God's will is done, wherever the love of God is manifested. The kingdom is yet to come in its fullness. But God's glorifying grace will bring to completion God's final reign of righteousness, which is God's power over evil and death.

Grace incorporates us into God's reign over sin and death and calls us to participate in God's transforming of creation. One United Methodist scholar writes, "This is what sanctification is all about— becoming an agent of the age to come, joining in the struggle against the forces of sin and corruption, claiming the promise of the new age and living in the hope that the victory over sin is indeed possible."[22]

It was this holistic understanding of salvation by grace that propelled the Methodists into evangelical mission and social action. Since their origin, Methodists have been involved in education, medical care, economic and political issues, and human rights concerns because of God's grace which seeks to bring into being a whole new creation. Wesley's involvement in issues of poverty, slavery, prison reform, human rights, education, and medical care did not result from a political agenda or as mere happenstance. His involvement grew out of his evangelical vision of God's grace, which transforms all of life, and his confidence in the ultimate triumph of God's realm.

CONCLUSION

The distinctive Wesleyan emphasis upon salvation by grace spawned a spiritual revival in eighteenth century England and on the American frontier. The message of God's universal grace present and available to all persons struck a responsive note among people who had been demoralized by their own sin and the sin of society. The poor and outcasts especially found hope, renewal, and transformation in the message that God the Creator who is for and with them will enable them to share in Christ's final victory over sin and death. God's prevenient, justifying, and sanctifying grace gave the Methodists their mission: to reform the nation, particularly the church, and to spread scriptural holiness throughout the land. By God's grace made flesh in Jesus Christ, they shared in the life and mission of God!

The world desperately needs the emphasis upon prevenient, justifying, and sanctifying grace. A generation that defines people by wealth, social status, academic degrees, professional achievements, physical appearance, and political power seeks wholeness (salvation) through having, doing, knowing, succeeding. The result is a secular form of "works righteousness" and its resulting despair and anxiety.

We need the affirmation that God has acted decisively in Jesus Christ to set us free from all idols and through the Holy Spirit continuously works to restore our identity as children of God. No longer do we have to earn our place in the world or prove our right to be. God has given us a place in God's own family and a part in God's mission to the world. In Jesus Christ, the divine image has been restored. We now share in the restored image. We are surrounded by grace—God's unmerited favor—which prods, prompts, forgives, and perfects us in love.

Prevenient, justifying, and sanctifying grace are not sequential or chronological experiences. Neither are they one-time manifestations of grace. Every moment is filled with all three dimensions of grace. Each prompting of prevenient grace leads to new gifts of forgiveness and acceptance, and every growth toward holiness or perfection drives us to deeper dimensions of God's love. By grace, we have been saved! By grace, we are being saved! By grace, we shall be saved to the utmost!

Opportunities for Reflection

The following questions may be used by groups wishing to discuss the material in chapter six or by individuals wanting to reflect on issues raised within the chapter.

1. "Grace pervades our understanding of Christian faith and life," affirms *The Book of Discipline*. Do you see this emphasis in your local congregation? The denomination? Share examples.
2. How would you describe the role that grace plays in your life?
3. In what way does our society value works rather than grace?
4. What are the implications of God's grace for our involvement in such issues as prison reform, economic justice, welfare reform, and the like?

7

Living and Growing in Grace

From his childhood years in an Anglican rectory until his death at the age of almost eighty-eight, John Wesley's life was characterized by personal discipline as a means of and response to grace. His disciplined, methodical pursuit of "holiness of heart and life"[1] accounts for the name "Methodist" being attached to Wesley and his followers. Although Wesley never particularly liked the term, it describes an important dimension of the Wesleyan understanding of Christian discipleship. Although the term was first used disparagingly, "Methodist" does express the profound truth that Christian living involves intentional, persistent, and disciplined practices in community with other Christians.

Grace as Gift and Response

While at Oxford University, Wesley was involved with a group of people who shared his commitment to disciplined Christian living. The group was referred to as the Oxford Methodists or "the Holy Club." In addition to devoting themselves to study, prayer, self-examination, and mutual admonition, they visited prisons twice each week, spent an hour or two every week in visiting the sick, and regularly ministered to and with the poor. They resolved to do good to as many people as possible and to refrain from all forms of sin. Wesley's motive for such rigorous pursuit of holiness changed from an effort to earn God's love and forgiveness to living in response to God's grace. Yet, obedience, discipline, and accountability remained integral components of the Methodist understanding and practice of discipleship.

Our identity as children of God is God's gift to us; living in the world as redeemed sons and daughters of God is our gift to God. Living the *imago Dei* and growing toward perfection in love involves accepting the grace of God *and* keeping covenant with God. Justifying grace reconciles us to God and sets us on the journey, and sanctifying grace forms us in the mind of Christ and sheds the love of God abroad in our hearts, actions, and relationships.

The response to Jesus' gracious invitation, "Come, follow me" (Matthew 4:19), begins a lifelong relationship of obedience and covenant faithfulness. Just as maintaining the marriage covenant requires sensitive and loving deeds as well as avoiding the temptations to unfaithfulness, maintaining covenant with Jesus Christ requires acts of devotion and obedience in addition to avoiding known sin.

Ours is an age that emphasizes feelings—subjectivity—especially in matters pertaining to religion and morality. Relationships, including with God, are judged primarily by the feelings they generate. Love is defined as physical attraction or warm feelings toward another. The validity and authenticity of religious beliefs and experiences are determined by their emotional intensity. One person said to me, "If you don't feel forgiven and saved, you haven't been." Or, behavior is often justified with the simple explanation, "It feels right." Feelings of certainty, optimism, excitement, serenity or "peace of mind" become the goals and tests of religious devotion.

While valuing and affirming feelings and emotions, Methodism has never defined Christian discipleship as subjective feeling. Being Christian is being conformed into the likeness of Jesus Christ. It is exhibiting the fruits of the Spirit, nothing less than holiness of heart and life, being made perfect in love. Discipleship in the Methodist tradition is both an art and a craft. It includes passion born of God's grace and it involves practices and habits that form us in love for God and neighbor.

Faith and Obedience

The Book of Discipline states: "We see God's grace and human activity working together in the relationship of faith and good works. God's grace calls forth human response and discipline. Faith is the only response essential for salvation. However . . . salvation evidences itself in good works."[2] It further affirms, "The coherence of faith with ministries of love forms the discipline of Wesleyan spirituality and Christian discipleship."[3] The doctrinal standards in the United Methodist tradition affirm good works as the fruits and manifestations of vital faith.

Methodism has always challenged those who would separate faith from obedience, or faith from works. In Wesley's own time, some religious groups believed that acts of obedience prior to a sense of personal assurance of salvation were "but splendid sins."[4] They believed that one could only wait quietly for a "religious experience" and then obedience would be possible. Wesley strongly disagreed with such a position. He urged the Methodists to trample "under foot that enthusiastic doctrine that 'we are not to do good unless our hearts be free to it.'"[5]

Wesley's conviction of the inseparability of faith and obedience grew out of his own experience. Before his experience of justification at Aldersgate Street, Wesley had concluded that he should cease preaching. He lacked a sense of assurance and certainty. He declared to the Moravian, Peter Böhler, that he had no faith. Wesley's inclusion in his Journal of Böhler's response is indicative of its importance in his faith journey: "Preach faith till you have it, and then, because you have it, you will preach faith."[6] As Wesley followed Böhler's advice, his faith and assurance increased. He concluded that there are degrees of faith; and increased obedience leads to growth in faith.

Obedience does not earn us forgiveness and reconciliation with God; but obedience is necessary to maintain the relationship with God. Married couples may contend that love is necessary in order for them to remain faithful to one another. It is equally true that faithfulness to one another is necessary in order to keep love alive and growing. An assurance of God's love and forgiveness is the ground of Christian discipleship, but obedience to Jesus Christ is necessary in order for the ground to produce a harvest.

Rather than being passive mental assent to a proposition or idea, faith is acting based on what God has done in Jesus Christ. It is being faithful to the promises and commands of Christ, regardless of feelings and consequences. Faith is obeying Christ's teachings, going where he commands, and welcoming those whom he loves, trusting that the Holy Spirit will guide and empower us each step of the way. With each act of obedience, faith is strengthened and additional guidance is given. Passively waiting for divine guidance and personal assurance is not faith in the Methodist understanding. Acting in accordance with the teachings and example of Jesus Christ both produces and manifests faith.

For United Methodists, the Christian life is an ongoing, dynamic pilgrimage toward total restoration of the divine image. It is the endless journey into holiness or perfect love. The journey involves following the commands of God, receiving forgiveness and restoration for failing to follow, and—out of gratitude for the forgiveness and restoration— striving all the more to be obedient.

Three Rules for Christian Disciples

Obedience requires understanding and trusting who Jesus Christ is and following him. We have to admit that some terrible things are done in the name of obedience to Jesus Christ. History is replete with examples of misdirected obedience—children sacrificed, mass suicides, racial hatred and violence, religious intolerance and persecution, psychological repression, physical abuse, to name but a few. Christ's name has been invoked on behalf of causes that the Jesus of the New Testament would never sanction. It is important, therefore, that guidelines for obedience to Christ be followed.

For United Methodists, the basic guideline is love for God and neighbor. The heart of the Christian way of life, according to John Wesley, is comprised in the Sermon on the Mount. The standard is always conformity to the image of Christ, who is the incarnation of perfect love. Inward holiness (our love for God) prompts outward holiness (our love of neighbor). Faith active in love is the essence of Christian living.

The pattern for Christian living in the Methodist tradition is set forth in the "General Rules for the United Societies." The only requirement for admission in the societies, as noted previously, was "a desire to flee from the wrath to come, and to be saved from their sins." However, continuation in the societies required that the members demonstrate their desire for salvation, "First, by doing no harm, by avoiding evil of every kind . . . Secondly, by doing good; by being in every kind merciful after their power; as they have opportunity, doing good of every possible sort, and, as far as possible, to all men . . . Thirdly, by attending upon all the ordinances of God."[7]

Early Methodists believed that these General Rules provided a basic pattern for Christian living and growing in grace. Rueben Job writes of the power of the General Rules:

> There are three simple rules that have the power to change the world. While they are ancient, they have seldom been fully put to test. But when and where practiced, the world of things as they were was shaken until a new formation, a new world was formed. The Wesleyan movement is a prime example of this new creation that is formed when these three simple rules are adopted as a way of living.[8]

Indeed, these rules and being held accountable for living them are at the heart of the Wesleyan revival in the eighteenth century.

MAKING ROOM FOR GRACE BY DOING NO HARM

The first rule is simple: Do no harm. It is the first principle of medical ethics and it is an appropriate initial consideration in making any decision or taking any action: Refrain from hurting or doing damage. We grow in grace as we refrain from indulging in that which harms ourselves, others, and the world. Wesley's list of evil and harm to be avoided included taking the Lord's name in vain, profaning the Lord's day, drunkenness, slaveholding, fighting and quarreling, dishonest advertising, wealthy display, charging high interest, violating the "Golden Rule," doing anything that does not "glorify God." The list may need to be updated by contemporary United Methodists, but the world would be a different place and we would be different people if the spiritual descendants of the early Methodists methodically sought to do no harm and to avoid evil of every kind and if we would hold one another accountable for the harm we do.

LIVING GRACE-FULLY BY "DOING GOOD"

Secondly, we evidence our response to grace "By doing good; by being in every kind merciful after [our] power; as [we] have opportunity, doing good of every possible sort, and, as far as possible, to all [people]."

Following Jesus Christ involves more than refraining from doing harm; it includes positively contributing to the well-being of others. Grace is God's love in action and the ultimate work of grace is to make us grace-full, full of grace. The primary mark of grace-fullness is generosity of spirit and action. Early Methodists interpreted "doing good" as including ministry to the physical, spiritual, economic, and educational needs of others and doing that which glorifies God. Visiting the sick and imprisoned, assisting the poor, providing employment and medical care, and enduring persecution for the gospel's sake were but some of the ways the Methodists were to do good.

Wesley considered acts of mercy to be as essential to Christian living as acts of piety, such as prayer, Bible reading, worship, and the sacraments. The Methodists considered visitation of the poor and imprisoned, care for at-risk children, aid to the sick, comfort to the hurting, and relief to the oppressed as integral to Christian discipleship and necessary spiritual disciplines. Such acts of mercy were considered as means of sharing in the life and mission of God, who defends the orphans, the widows, and the strangers.

Since God is especially present among the suffering and the vulnerable, we experience God's presence and grace as we share friendship and aid with the marginalized. Wesley was convinced that authentic religion goes from the weak to the powerful rather than from the powerful to the weak. Otherwise, we assume that salvation results from our own power and ingenuity. We cannot share communion with God and fulfill the divine image apart from sharing the life of the poor and the vulnerable by doing good with them and all people.

GROWING IN GRACE BY "ATTENDING UPON ALL THE ORDINANCES OF GOD"

The third means by which we live and grow in grace is by "attending upon all the ordinances of God." Rueben Job renames this rule as "Stay in love with God."[9] By "ordinance" Wesley meant the practices that nurture our understanding of and relationship with God. Cultivating relationship with and love for God requires practices that sensitize us to the reality and presence of God. Such "acts of piety" as personal devotions, Bible study, corporate worship, and theological reflection are means of practicing the presence of God and nurturing friendship with Christ.

More will be said about these ordinances in the next chapter as we focus on means of grace. Growing in faith requires the nurturing of our spiritual lives through worship, participation in the Sacraments, prayer, Bible study, and spiritual disciplines, such as fasting.

Moral and ethical integrity, service to others, and spiritual formation are general rules of Christian discipleship. Faith includes obedience to Jesus Christ—acts of compassion and justice as well as acts of personal devotion and worship. Faith and obedience involve self-discipline and individual effort. Accountability is also a necessary ingredient of Christian discipleship.

Grace as Being Held in Love and Being Held Accountable

Discipleship in the Wesleyan tradition includes living in covenant and accountability. The class meetings and other small groups were integral to the early Methodist movement. It was in the class meetings that the Methodists were held accountable for their growth in grace and discipleship. There were about twelve people in each class, with one designated the leader. The underlying purpose of the class meetings was "to watch over one another in love." The class leader was responsible to see each person in the class at least once a week, "in order (1) to inquire how their souls prosper; (2) to advise, reprove, comfort or exhort, as occasion may require; (3) to receive what they are willing to give toward the relief of preachers, church, and poor."[10]

In the weekly gatherings, as Wesley said, "a more full inquiry was made into the behaviour of every person . . . advice or reproof was given as need required, quarrels made up, misunderstandings removed; and after an hour or two spent in this labour of love, they concluded with prayer and thanksgiving."[11] In the bands, which consisted of those people who had justifying grace and were more seriously pursuing holiness of heart and life, participants were expected to share more in depth their struggles to be obedient and faithful. The following questions were asked in the weekly band meetings:

1. What known sins have you committed since our last meeting?
2. What temptations have you met with?
3. How were you delivered?
4. What have you thought, said, or done, of which you doubt whether it be sin or not?
5. Have you nothing you desire to keep secret?[12]

Accountability has traditionally been a hallmark of discipleship among United Methodists. However, individualism and the popular notion that we are innately good and, when left alone, will develop naturally into whole and honorable people have eroded accountability and discipline even among United Methodists. Personal autonomy and individual freedom of choice are seen as the means to self-actualization and fulfillment. Discipleship is reduced to following one's own individual conscience and pious passions, with little reference to accountability to the larger community of faith.

Alcoholics Anonymous and other groups that seek to free people from addictions demonstrate the importance of being part of a community of support and accountability. Members are drawn together by their awareness of their common condition and need for help in breaking the power of addiction. With the aid and support of a sponsor, they confront their vulnerabilities and temptations, tell their stories, and hold one another accountable for sobriety. The "Twelve Steps" are foundational rules for psychic awakening and growth in sobriety, and they come together regularly to examine, confess, support, and thereby find relief from the bondage to addiction.

Wesley and the early Methodists knew that holiness of heart and life, or entire love for God and neighbor, requires a community of support and accountability. We are addicted to sin and cannot break the addiction apart from a community in which we are held in love and held accountable. Methodists have always affirmed the importance of conversion and power of the Holy Spirit to transform our hearts and desires, what Wesley called "tempers." However, Wesley and the early Methodist leaders resisted the notion that conversion removed all desire to sin and he insisted that growth in grace requires disciplines in the context of supportive community.

God's presence and power to heal, forgive, reconcile, and transform (grace) hold us in love and hold us accountable. The early Methodists gathered in small groups weekly to watch over one another in love. Through those small groups, they held one another in love and held one another accountable for doing no harm, doing good, and engaging in practices that enabled them to grow in grace and discipleship.

Grace, Discipline, and Christian Freedom

Disciplines and accountability are often resisted in our culture as infringements on freedom. Freedom, or liberty, has come to mean the ability to pursue limitless options without impunity. Freedom is the removal of restraints. Some interpret grace as setting us free from demands and expectations. Dietrich Bonhoeffer called such interpretation as "cheap grace" which he defined this way:

> Cheap grace is the preaching of forgiveness without requiring repentance, baptism without church discipline, Communion without confession, absolution without personal confession.

Cheap grace is grace without discipleship, grace without the cross, grace without Jesus Christ, living and incarnate.[13]

Indeed, Christ sets us free; but it is a freedom different from license to pursue unlimited options. As Paul writes to the Galatians, "For freedom Christ has set us free . . . For you were called to freedom, brothers and sisters; only do not use your freedom as an opportunity for self-indulgence, but through love become slaves to one another" (5:1,13). Christian freedom includes avoiding such things as "fornication, impurity, licentiousness, idolatry, sorcery, enmities, strife, jealousy, anger, quarrels, dissensions, factions, envy, drunkenness, carousing . . ." (Galatians 5:19-21). Freedom is yoking ourselves to Christ so that the Holy Spirit produces in us such fruits as "love, joy, peace, patience, kindness, generosity, faithfulness, gentleness, and self-control" (Galatians 5:22-23).

Christian freedom is more like the freedom of an Olympic athlete or concert musician. The freedom of an Olympic gymnast to gracefully perform on the parallel bars has been gained through years of discipline and practice. Only the pianist who has mastered the musical scales and practiced endless hours has the freedom to play a Chopin sonata. Only those who cultivate and practice doing no harm, doing good, and cultivating love for God and neighbor are free to exhibit the fruit of the Spirit—love, joy, peace, patience, kindness, generosity, faithfulness, gentleness, and self-control.

Discipleship in the Methodist understanding is a craft requiring persistent use and practice. A craft is learned through apprenticeship and developed through constant use. No one is free to be a craftsperson if he or she is unwilling to pay the price to master the necessary skills. A love for the craft is a prerequisite, but being a craftsperson involves disciplined and persistent following of guidelines, rules, and principles. The craft of Christian discipleship includes a love for the one the disciples called "Master," a willingness to follow the rules and guidelines set forth in the teachings and example of Christ, and relationships in which we are held accountable for living our beliefs.

Charles Wesley's hymn expresses the relationship between grace, discipline, and a supportive community of accountability:

Help us to help each other,
Lord, each other's cross to bear;
let all their friendly aid afford,
and feel each other's care.

Up unto thee, our living Head,
let us in all things grow;
till thou hast made us free indeed,
and spotless here below.

Touched by the lodestone of thy love,
let all our hearts agree,
and ever toward each other move,
and ever move toward thee.

To thee, inseparably joined,
let all our spirits cleave;
O may we all the loving mind
that was in thee receive.[14]

Conclusion

Christian discipleship is a journey toward maturity in Christ, requiring a lifetime of discipline and accountability. The traditional Methodist emphasis upon growth in grace and discipleship through obedience and accountability has waned in recent years. Discipline and accountability have given way to individualism, personal autonomy, and libertinism as means to personal fulfillment. One result is new forms of bondage, bondage to personal ambition and appetites, conformity to societal expectations, and captivity to culturally defined images of success.

Early Methodists represented an alternative way of life to the self-indulgence, hedonism, and social fragmentation of their society. Alternatives to the narcissism, consumerism, and hedonism of contemporary living are desperately needed. Discipleship characterized by commitment to the rule of love for God and neighbor within the context of a community in which we are held and held accountable is the Methodist means to authentic freedom. In Jesus Christ, God has held us in love; in Jesus Christ, we are called into a covenantal relationship;

and through the Holy Spirit at work in community, we are given power to live in obedience.

Methodists traditionally have participated in an annual Covenant Service. The prayer used in that service proclaims the life of discipleship to which the "people called Methodists" aspire and which grace makes possible:

I am no longer my own, but thine.

Put me to what thou wilt, rank me with whom thou wilt.

Put me to doing, put me to suffering.

Let me be employed by thee or laid aside for thee, exalted for thee or brought low by thee.

Let me be full, let me be empty.
Let me have all things, let me have nothing.
I freely and heartily yield all things
to thy pleasure and disposal.
And now, O glorious and blessed God,
Father, Son, and Holy Spirit,
thou art mine, and I am thine. So be it.
And the covenant which I have made on earth,
let it be ratified in heaven. Amen.[15]

Opportunities for Reflection

The following questions may be used by groups wishing to discuss the material in chapter seven or by individuals wanting to reflect on issues raised within the chapter.

1. How would you define the relationship between grace and discipline? Faith and works? What difference is there between doing no harm and doing good in order to earn grace, and avoiding evil and doing good in response to having accepted God's grace?

2. Wesley was specific in identifying harm to be avoided and good to be done. You may want to review his list and discuss their relevancy today. If you were making a list of harm to be avoided and good to be done today, what would you include?

3. What are your reactions to the early Methodist class meetings and bands? Have you been part of a group in which members were vulnerable about their own struggles and temptations and open to being held accountable by the group? Does your local church have small groups similar to the class meetings? Accountable Discipleship is a program in The United Methodist Church that assists in the formation of covenant discipleship groups. You may wish to be part of that program.

4. What is your definition of "freedom"? Discuss the image of Christian freedom as being similar to the freedom of an accomplished athlete or concert musician. Do you agree that discipline and accountability are necessary if we are to be free to love God and neighbor? In what ways do discipline and accountability produce freedom?

8

Means of Grace—Nurturing Relationship with God

Sharing God's life and mission through Christian discipleship is a journey toward perfection in love, or holiness of heart and life. Growing in the image of Christ requires faith manifested and strengthened in obedience. Jesus' command, "Come, follow me," is an invitation to share in a transforming friendship with Jesus Christ and an unending pilgrimage toward the kingdom of God, the reign of righteousness. Following Christ is often dangerous, exhausting, and costly. The journey takes us through wildernesses of temptation, valleys of suffering and struggle, mountain peaks of lofty visions, gardens of anguish, hillsides of crucifixion, and tombs of death and grief.

Growing in grace and discipleship cannot be done within our own strength. The good news is that the One who invites us on the journey accompanies us and supplies our needs. The God who liberates us and gives us a new future enables us to live toward our new destiny. God freed the Hebrew people, shaped them into a new people, and led them through the desert into the Promised Land. The God who commanded the people to move forward went before them and provided food for their journey. The law given to Moses, the tabernacle that went before the people, the manna in the wilderness, and leaders such as Moses and Miriam were all means of grace or resources for the journey.

In Jesus Christ, we have been set free from bondage to sin and incorporated into Christ's present and future reign of compassion, justice, peace, generosity, and joy. We have been called and sent on our way to a new destiny, the kingdom of God. Living toward that new future requires resources we do not have within ourselves. The One who calls us, however, is the one who accompanies us and provides food for the journey.

Discipleship in the United Methodist tradition is a process of growth in our awareness of and response to the power and presence of God. Growth requires nourishment and exercise. The General Rules of the Societies and the accountability experienced in the class meetings and bands provided sustenance for those seeking to grow in their discipleship. Methodists, since their beginning, have identified the ordinances of God as means of grace—channels of God's presence and power to heal, forgive, and transform. Attendance upon the ordinances of God was required for continued membership in the early Methodist societies because they provided indispensable food for the pilgrimage toward personal and social holiness. They were and are means by which we nurture our relationship with God, or as Rueben Job says, "stay in love with God."[1]

God's presence is not self-evident in our hectic, secularized, and technology-dominated world. A culture that looks to science, technology, economics, and politics for answers to perplexing questions and solutions to thorny problems has little room for mystery, reverence, and awe. Cultivating and practicing the presence of God has always required intentionality and disciplines. Today, the challenge is even more daunting, making the means of grace, or the ordinances of God, even more crucial for those who desire holiness of heart and life.

The following are means of grace for United Methodists as specifically named in the General Rules:[2]

- The public worship of God
- The ministry of the Word, either read or expounded
- The Supper of the Lord
- Family and private prayer
- Searching the scriptures
- Fasting or abstinence

Additionally, John Wesley identified "Christian conference" as an "instituted" means of grace.[3]

As noted in the previous chapter, avoiding evil and doing works of mercy and justice, especially ministry with the poor, are also means of grace. Obedience is in response to sharing in God's life and mission in Jesus Christ, not the precondition for salvation. The ordinances of the church are therefore to be seen as nourishment for disciples on their way to the new heaven and new earth. They are means of living in God's presence and thereby growing in the mind of Christ.

Public Worship

The following is an affirmation of the meaning and importance of public worship as contained in our doctrinal standards:

> We believe divine worship is the duty and privilege of man [humanity] who, in the presence of God, bows in adoration, humility, and dedication. We believe divine worship is essential to the life of the Church, and that the assembling of the people of God for such worship is necessary to Christian fellowship and spiritual growth.[4]

Methodism was birthed and nurtured in the rich liturgical life of the Anglican Church. Although the Methodist movement was centered in the class meetings and in the open fields where the masses heard preached the gospel of prevenient, justifying, and sanctifying grace, worship in the parish church was expected. Gathering regularly to share praise, confession, the Lord's Supper, and the Word read and proclaimed was considered foundational for Christian living.

Worship literally means "to declare worth." In worship, we declare the worth of God through acts of praise, confession, listening, and giving.

The focus of worship is the reality and presence of God, not our own needs or desires. Worship differs from entertainment in that God is the audience and we are the performers. Our music, prayers, attentiveness, and dedication are gifts we bring to the transcendent God who graciously enters into communion with us. We hold our lives alongside the holy, righteous, and loving God. In the presence of the One who is love and holiness, we are "lost in wonder, love and praise."[5] In the presence of perfect love and goodness, we are aware of our failure in love and our brokenness, and we cry out for forgiveness and reconciliation. In response to God's presence and assurance of forgiveness, we listen for God's Word and commit ourselves to it. In this regular rehearsal of our relationship with God in Christ, windows into grace are opened to us and we are fed by the living Christ through the Holy Spirit.

Worship is a corporate act. We gather as the body of Christ and by our presence together we affirm that the risen Christ is with us. Rather than gathering as an audience to individually enjoy or critique the performance, we come together to jointly share in God's joy and God's critique of us. We help one another praise, confess, affirm faith, receive the divine Word, and offer commitments. Therefore, worship is not judged by "what I get out of it" or the "friendliness of the people." Worship's effectiveness is judged by the integrity of what the gathered community offers to God.

The form of worship services varies among United Methodists. The style of the music, order of the service, and degree of formality depend upon the cultural context and traditions of the community. The basic pattern of worship is framed around Word and Table and includes the following:

- gathering in the Lord's name through prayer and praise;
- proclamation and response;
- thanksgiving and communion; and
- sending forth into the world.[6]

We are shaped by whatever we consider worthy of praise, confession, and imitation. Gathering in the name and presence of the risen Christ, expressing our praise and confession to the holy and loving God, hearing the Word proclaimed and responding to it, and sharing thanksgiving and communion with one another and Jesus Christ are all vehicles by which the Holy Spirit comes to us and enables us to grow toward the image of God. Public worship is a means by which we practice the presence of God and grow in friendship with Jesus Christ through the power of the Holy Spirit.

The Sacraments

Central to Christian worship are the Sacraments. *The Book of Discipline* states:

> We believe the Sacraments, ordained by Christ, are symbols and pledges of the Christian's profession and of God's love toward us. They are means of grace by which God works invisibly in us, quickening, strengthening, and confirming our faith in him. Two Sacraments are ordained by Christ our Lord, namely Baptism and the Lord's Supper.[7]

The Sacraments are visible acts, initiated by Christ, in which the Triune God claims, reconciles, and transforms us. Through Baptism and Communion we are incorporated into Christ's body and called into ministry. We share Christ's ongoing life, death, resurrection, and final victory.

BAPTISM

Baptism is initiation into the family of God, cleansing from sin, and a sign of new birth as children of God, claimed and empowered by the Holy Spirit for mission in the world. Our doctrinal standards include this affirmation: "We believe Baptism signifies entrance into the household of faith, and is a symbol of repentance and inner cleansing from sin, a representation of the new birth in Christ Jesus and a mark of Christian discipleship."[8]

Baptism is our birthmark as sons and daughters of God and our initiation into God's household. It is a declaration of God's initiative in claiming us as beloved children, cleansing and redeeming us, and empowering us to share in the divine mission in the world. Baptism celebrates what God has done, is doing, and shall do on our behalf. It is entrance into Christ's community, the Church; therefore, the community shares in covenant with each baptized person. Since baptism represents God's initiative in claiming, redeeming, and incorporating us into the Christian community, rebaptism and private baptisms are inappropriate.

"We believe children are under the atonement of Christ and as heirs of the Kingdom of God are acceptable subjects for Christian baptism."[9] Neither our identity as children of God and members of Christ's community nor God's forgiving and reconciling action in Jesus Christ are age related. Therefore, United Methodists baptize infants and people of all ages. The baptism of infants especially affirms God's claim upon us before our own response. The baptism of infants is not to be confused with christening, the giving of a name, or a dedication by the parents. Infant baptism means the same as adult baptism. All baptisms are covenant services in which the community—the church—promises to nurture and support the baptized in living their God-given identity and fulfilling their individual and corporate ministries.

United Methodists consider three modes of baptism equally valid: sprinkling, pouring, and immersion. The three modes have been practiced throughout church history. They carry the same meaning but with special emphases. Sprinkling places an emphasis on cleansing; pouring reminds us of the bestowing of the Holy Spirit; and immersion signifies the burial of the old self and the rising of the new. Cleansing from sin, the pouring upon us of the Holy Spirit, and the gift of new life are dimensions of baptism whatever the mode used. Baptism is a gift of God by which we are born into a new identity, a new community, and a new destiny.

HOLY COMMUNION

Charles and John Wesley recognized the power of God present in the Lord's Supper and they urged the Methodists to draw on that power by frequent participation. John Wesley himself participated in the sacrament an average of four to five times a week. He described the Lord's Supper as "the grand channel whereby the grace of his Spirit was conveyed to the souls of all the children of God,"[10] and the Wesleys emphasized through their sermons and hymns that through Holy

Communion we experience love, forgiveness, the presence of Christ, mystery, healing, holiness, and a foretaste of heaven.

The Book of Discipline declares that the Lord's Supper (Holy Communion, or the Eucharist) is "a representation of our redemption, a memorial of the sufferings and death of Christ, and a token of love and union that Christians have with Christ and with one another."[11] It is a participation in the life, death, and resurrection of Jesus Christ and an anticipation of Christ's final victory over sin and death. In remembering Jesus—his birth, life, teachings, death, and resurrection—and in partaking of symbols of his broken body and shed blood, the crucified, risen, and glorified Christ is present with us.

In Holy Communion, we share our oneness with Christ, with one another, and with the Christians who have gone before us. We declare, "Because there is one loaf, we, who are many, are one body, for we all partake of the one loaf. The bread which we break is a sharing in the body of Christ. The cup over which we give thanks is a sharing in the blood of Christ."[12] Because the supper is Christ's Supper and not our own, all are invited to share in it. The Invitation affirms: "Christ our Lord invites to his table all who love him, and earnestly repent of their sin and seek to live in peace with one another."[13]

John Wesley urged Methodists to share in the Lord's Supper at least weekly. He believed that regular sharing in the Supper of the Lord provided indispensable nourishment for the soul. Few United Methodists celebrate Holy Communion weekly, although a growing number of churches offer the sacrament every Sunday. The General Conference of 2004 approved *This Holy Mystery: A United Methodist Understanding of Holy Communion* in which it is strongly recommended that congregations move toward weekly celebration of the Lord's Supper.[14]

Some people hesitate to participate in the sacrament because they feel unworthy. The feeling of unworthiness is all the more reason to participate, for Holy Communion is the celebration of God's action in making us worthy. Regular participation in the sacrament provides a rehearsal and foretaste of the heavenly banquet when the faithful "come from the east and west and will eat with Abraham and Isaac and Jacob in the kingdom of heaven" (Matthew 8:11).

Acts of Personal Devotion

In addition to public worship and the sacraments, acts of personal devotion are means of grace in the Wesleyan tradition. Private and public prayer, searching the scriptures, and fasting are important avenues of growth in discipleship and expressions of faithfulness to Christ. Through such disciplines, we hold our lives in the presence of God and receive guidance and strength for our walk with Christ in the world. They are means by which we cultivate friendship with Christ, grow toward Christ's likeness, and serve Christ in the world. Rueben Job writes:

> Living in the presence of and in harmony with the living God who is made known in Jesus Christ and companions us in the Holy Spirit is to live life from the inside out. It is to find our moral direction, our wisdom, our courage, our strength to live faithfully from the One who authored us, called us, sustains us, and sends us into the world as witnesses.[15]

PRIVATE AND PUBLIC PRAYER

Methodism was born and nurtured in the discipline of private and public prayer. Throughout his life, John Wesley followed a strict regimen of daily prayer. His day began and ended with prayer, and every hour included pause for prayers of thanksgiving. Other than the Bible, the *Anglican Book of Common Prayer* was the book most used by Wesley. He regularly participated in the Services of Morning and Evening Prayers and many of the prayers of the church had been committed to memory. Prayer was an integral part of every meeting of the societies and classes. He proclaimed in his sermon, "The Means of Grace," "All who desire the grace of God are to wait for it in the way of prayer. This is the express direction of our Lord himself."[16]

Prayer is communion with God, practicing the presence of God. Through focusing our thoughts upon God, expressing our feelings and dreams and needs to God, and seeking guidance, the transcendent One becomes the immanent One, the holy other becomes a holy presence. Traditional forms of prayer include thanksgiving and praise, petition, and confession. Expressing gratitude and adoration to God lifts us toward transcendent beauty, truth, goodness, and love. Petitions and intercessions are resources that God uses in God's own time and way for the advancement of the divine kingdom. Through confession, we admit our sin, request forgiveness, and accept assurance of divine forgiveness. Prayer, therefore, is as indispensable for spiritual health as regular meals are for physical health. It is a means of cultivating friendship with the Risen Christ through the Holy Spirit.

SEARCHING THE SCRIPTURES

Searching the scriptures is a means by which God's grace guides, shapes, and directs us. Our doctrinal standards include the following affirmation of the central role the Bible plays in our discipleship:

> We believe the Holy Bible, Old and New Testaments, reveals the Word of God so far as it is necessary for our salvation. It is to be received through the Holy Spirit as the true rule and guide for faith and practice. Whatever is not revealed in or established by the Holy Scriptures is not to be made an article of faith nor is it to be taught as essential to salvation.[17]

Sharing in God's life and mission involves an understanding of the divine nature and will. Being shaped by God's nature and purpose requires constant, disciplined exposure to God's self-disclosure. The Bible bears witness to God's being and action in history. It is the story of God's relationship with creation and God's initiatives in seeking to bring to completion the divine purpose of all existence. The scriptures, however, are more than reports of past events; they are a means of God's revelation and presence to the people of God in the here and now.

By searching the scriptures, learning the stories of faith, wrestling with their meaning, looking for a Word from the Lord, God comes walking from the pages of the Bible and into our mind and spirit. Through its varied kinds of literature and multiple historical and cultural contexts, the Bible communicates the eternal Word for our time.

John Wesley referred to himself as *homo unius libri*—a man of "one book."[18] He affirmed that it contains all things necessary for salvation, and United Methodists consider scripture as the primary source of God's revelation. Wesley was so familiar with the Bible that its stories, images, and expressions were like a second language. He spent time every day in prayerful study of the scriptures and expected Methodist preachers and class leaders to do the same. His *Explanatory Notes Upon the New Testament* became required reading for early Methodist leaders.

Searching the scriptures is a personal and communal discipline. Reading the Bible is a personal act in which we engage prayerfully and with openness to the Holy Spirit. Individual study of the scriptures— and employing interpretive tools such as commentaries—is a means of growth in discipleship. The use of daily readings from the Revised Common Lectionary and *The Upper Room Daily Devotional Guide* can lead to new insights and assurances of the divine presence.

It is important to remember that the Bible is the church's book and it is to be read in community. Individual interpretations must be subjected to the interpretation of the broader Christian community. The early Methodist classes and societies devoted time to searching the scriptures and grappling with their implications. Contemporary United Methodists rediscover the value of studying the scriptures in community as Disciple Bible Study® classes, Sunday school groups, and other settings provide opportunities to explore with other disciples the divine Word found in the Holy Scriptures. Such groups provide both support for continuing exploration and accountability. Reading the Bible in community helps to avoid an individualistic interpretation which ignores its historic message and distorts its meaning.

FASTING

Fasting has been a part of Methodism from its early beginnings, and John Wesley personally fasted weekly. "The Wesley Fast," traditionally observed, began on Thursday evening and continued through teatime on Friday. The timing corresponded to Jesus' last meal with the disciples on Holy Thursday through his death on the cross on Good Friday. It was a time to identify with Jesus' suffering and death, reflect on and repent of our sin, enter solidarity with those who hunger, and deepen our relationship with Christ. John Wesley wrote: "Is not the neglect of this plain duty (I mean fasting, ranked by our Lord with thanksgiving and prayer) one general occasion of deadness among Christians? Can anyone willingly neglect it and be guiltless?"[19]

Fasting is deeply grounded in scripture and in the life and ministry of Jesus. Jesus opened his ministry with a forty-day fast corresponding to that of Moses (Matthew 4:2). He taught that fasting is service to God and a sign of true conversion to the kingdom of God (Matthew 9:14-17). In the Bible, fasting is often connected with prayer. It is a sign of repentance, mourning, and preparation for God's coming. Abstaining from food serves as a reminder of life's emptiness apart from God's presence and love and our dependence upon divine grace.

Few modern United Methodists practice fasting and abstinence as a spiritual discipline. Some engage in the discipline occasionally, perhaps during Lent. However, as an act of obedience or an expression of openness to the coming reign of God, fasting can deepen our relationship with Christ and remind us of Christ's presence with impoverished and suffering people. Marjorie Thompson, in her book *Soul Feast*, considers fasting a means of "self emptying" that opens us to God's nourishing presence:

> In a more tangible, visceral way than any other spiritual discipline, fasting reveals our excessive attachments and assumptions that lie behind them. Food is necessary to life, but we have made it more necessary than God. How often have we neglected to remember God's presence when we would never consider neglecting to eat! Fasting brings us face to face with how we put the material world ahead of its spiritual Source.[20]

CHRISTIAN CONFERENCE

Another traditional Methodist means of grace is Christian conference, or "right conversation." Wesley included Christian conference as an instituted means of grace. He rhetorically asked these questions in conjunction with Christian conference: "Are you convinced how important and how difficult it is to 'order our conversation right?' Is it 'always in grace'? seasoned with salt? meet [i.e., fit or appropriate] to minister grace to the hearers? Do not you converse too long at a time? Is not an hour commonly enough? Would it not be well to have a determinate end in view; and to pray before and after it?"[21]

The first "conference" was held in 1744 when Wesley gathered five leaders of the Methodist movement to consider basic doctrinal and missional concerns and strategies. They spent one full day discussing justification and a second day was devoted to sanctification. While the term "Christian conferencing" has come to be associated with annual conferences, charge conferences, and other official gatherings of Methodists, its primary form in the Wesleyan understanding is what we would simply call religious conversation. All conversations, whether within the family or Sunday school class or among co-workers, are potential means and expressions of grace.

Still, there is an important role for such gatherings as annual conferences and charge conferences. Wesley considered such communal conferences as indispensable means of discerning God's will, sharing in God's mission in the world, and connecting with other Methodists. In more recent years, however, United Methodist conferences have become more focused on administrative and business issues than on theological reflection, missional strategy, or spiritual discernment. They tend to be dominated by parliamentary procedure, committee reports, and organizational functions. The loss of the original intent of conferences has contributed to a blurring of theological vision and a weakening of missional power. Attempts are being made to recover more of the historic role and format of such conferences by including such components as Bible study, mission engagement, and framing the sessions around worship.

Conversation with other Christians around issues of faith and mission is a means by which God guides and strengthens us. Sharing our understandings and struggles with others who are seeking to participate in God's life and work opens new avenues of divine grace and guidance. Through such sharing, the Holy Spirit is present to direct, empower, and transform. Dialogue in an atmosphere of humility and respect is a form of evangelism and prophetic witness. Jesus promised, "For where two or three are gathered in my name, I am there among them" (Matthew 18:20). In the midst of honest discussion and through the power of the Holy Spirit, the risen Christ comes to provide food for our journey toward the fulfillment of God's purpose.

Conclusion

Discerning God's presence and guidance and living as disciples of Jesus Christ do not come naturally or easily in the modern world. Holiness of heart and life, being made perfect in love, and being a citizen of God's new heaven and new earth involves far more than a one-time experience of divine forgiveness. Salvation—the complete restoration of the divine image in us and in all creation—is a continuing process. Following Jesus Christ inevitably puts us at odds with the world as it is, and the struggle is both internal and external. Sin continues to stalk us and temptation never forsakes us. Principalities and powers in the form of political and economic realities and cultural expectations and practices constantly lure us away from loyalty to Christ. Sharing in the life of the world as it is, is easier than sharing in the life and work of God's world of justice, righteousness, generosity, and joy.

The God who calls us out of bondage and into a new world does not leave us alone in the wilderness. As God gave manna in the wilderness to the Hebrew slaves en route to the promised land, God provides food for our journey toward a world transformed by Jesus Christ. This food is a means of grace or an ordinance of God. Participation in these gifts of grace cultivates friendship with the One who goes before us as the source of our guidance and perseverance.

Public worship, participation in the Sacraments, private and public prayer, searching the scriptures, fasting, and Christian conferences are acts of devotion in the Wesleyan tradition. They are works by which we earn a relationship with Christ. They are gifts by which our lives are shaped by friendship with Christ. Through them, we express our devotion and open our lives to the presence and power of God. They become means by which we are fed the Bread of Life and grow in our love for God and neighbor.

Opportunities for Reflection

The following questions may be used by groups wishing to discuss the material in chapter eight or by individuals wanting to reflect on issues raised within the chapter.

1. "Why are we not more holy?" was a question to which John
   Wesley responded, "Chiefly because we are . . . looking for
   the ends without using the means." Discuss the question and
   Wesley's response in light of our society's expectations of
   quick, effortless results without discipline and accountability.
   In what ways do we expect the fruits of Christian living without discipline and accountability?

2. What is your response to the discussion of freedom and
   discipline? In what ways is Christian freedom similar to the
   freedom of a concert musician or accomplished athlete? Do
   such "fruits of the Spirit" as love, joy, peace, patience, kindness, and self-control (Galatians 5:22) require discipline,
   practice, and accountability? Why or why not?

3. How often does your congregation participate in Holy
   Communion? What do you think about observing the
   Lord's Supper weekly? Why do so? What are the obstacles
   to weekly observance?

4. As you consider the means of grace mentioned in this
   chapter, which have the most meaning for you? The most
   challenge? Why? Does your church offer covenant discipleship groups in which acts of devotion and acts of mercy are
   components of the covenant?

5. Have you attended a "charge conference" or an "annual conference"? If not, ask your pastor or lay member of annual
   conference to describe the sessions. What suggestions do
   you have for changing the sessions to reflect more closely
   the early Methodist conferences as a means of grace? How
   would you suggest that all gatherings in the church engage
   in "Christian conferencing"?

6. If charge conferences or annual conferences focused less on
   administrative/business issues and more on spiritual discernment or theological reflection, how might The United
   Methodist Church be affected?

7. In what ways are the spiritual disciplines (acts) discussed in
   this chapter really "food for the journey"?

9

Church: A Called and Committed People

John Wesley wrote in 1785: "How much do we almost continually hear about the Church! . . . And yet how few understand what they talk of! How few know what the term means! A more ambiguous word than this, the 'church,' is scarce to be found in the English language."[1] Today in America, churches exist in almost every neighborhood. A majority of people count themselves as church members. Yet, confusion abounds as to the nature and purpose of the church, even among those who participate regularly in its activities.

Critics contend that the church has lost its identity and reason for existence. What difference does the church make? How different, if any, would neighborhoods be if churches were not present? Disturbing studies indicate that people who belong to churches reflect the values, attitudes, and behavior of society. Once, the church was a major moral and ethical influence in society. Now, however, its voice on the issues of private and public morality has been marginalized or confined to a narrow political agenda.

Walter Brueggemann in his book *Biblical Perspectives on Evangelism* diagnoses the contemporary church's problem as amnesia.[2] The influential scholar contends that the church has lost its memory. It has forgotten what and whose it is. As a person with amnesia depends upon other people to define who he or she is, the church that does not know its own origin and destiny receives its identity from the world around it. Without a memory of what the church is called to be, the church becomes what people want it to be. The self-defined needs and wishes of the people become more influential than God's mission to the world. Sociological surveys, marketing strategies, and multiple option activities become tools more basic than doctrinal clarity, accountable discipleship, missional focus, and liturgical and theological integrity.

The church is treated as another voluntary organization that people join as they do a civic club or a political party. Loyalty is measured by frequency of attendance, payment of pledges, service on committees, and participation in activities. The church is considered to be something we belong to rather than someone we are. Membership and participation are viewed as optional, depending upon personal preferences and satisfaction. The church, then, is seen as another institution among many institutions competing for our time, energy, and financial resources. Its distinctiveness as a called people of God committed to being a sign, foretaste, and instrument of God's presence and power is lost amid institutional survival and personal satisfaction.

The church's identity and mission are rooted in God. As a community called into being for the purpose of participating in God's life and mission in the world, the church must live its divine identity and mission. The United Methodist Church's distinctive heritage and emphases provide resources for reclaiming and strengthening the church's transforming and redemptive presence in society.

Methodism's Beginning: Renewal Movement within the Church

Methodism began as a reform and renewal movement within the Church of England. John Wesley and the Methodists set out "to reform the nation, particularly the Church, and to spread scriptural holiness over the land."[3] Early Methodists wanted to spread in the hearts of people love for God and neighbor, not to establish a new church. Early Methodists continued to participate in the worship and sacramental life of the Anglican Church. Since members of the classes and societies were expected to share in worship at their parish churches, the early Methodist meetings were scheduled at times other than Sunday mornings. John and Charles Wesley maintained their status as priests in the Church of England. No Methodist Church was formed in England until after the death of John Wesley.

Methodists first formed themselves into an organized church in America. In 1784, the Methodist Episcopal Church was organized, but the emphasis on evangelization and mission continued to dominate the new church's self-understanding and structure. The basic doctrines were Wesley's adaptation of the Anglican Articles of Religion. American Methodists, like their counterparts in England, were occupied with proclaiming the gospel and forming disciples of Jesus Christ. The circuit riders traveled widely across the frontier and were often the first to greet the new settlers. They provided instruction, inspiration, and the sacraments during their visits in local communities. The center of congregational life remained in the class meetings, preaching houses, and revival meetings. Laity supplied the basic leadership, and class leaders and lay preachers provided ongoing pastoral care during the long periods between visits by the circuit riders. Organizational structures, buildings, and formalized doctrinal statements were less important than calling forth, teaching, nurturing, and supporting Christian disciples.

As American society became more organized and bureaucratized, so did the Methodist Church. Eventually, the circuit rider became the pastor of the local congregation. Buildings and organization took on added importance as the Methodist Church became the largest Protestant denomination in nineteenth- and early-twentieth-century America. Still, the origins as a reform and missional movement continued to shape the Methodist Church's life and work. Since Methodism did not begin as a result of doctrinal disputes or theological distinctiveness, that which gave the church identity was its mission to "reform the nation and spread scriptural holiness."

The Nature and Mission of the Church

Our doctrinal standards contain the following description of the church's identity and mission:

> We believe the Christian Church is the community of all true believers under the Lordship of Christ. We believe it is one, holy, apostolic and catholic. It is the redemptive fellowship in which the Word of God is preached by men [persons] divinely called, and the sacraments are duly administered according to Christ's own appointment. Under the discipline of the Holy Spirit the Church exists for the maintenance of worship, the edification of believers and the redemption of the world.[4]

The Book of Discipline affirms, "the mission of the Church is to make disciples of Jesus Christ for the transformation of the world."[5] It further states, "A grace-formed church is one which responsibly participates in God's action in and for the world. . . . This mission is our grace-filled response to the Reign of God in the world announced by Jesus."[6] The church is a people called into being by God to be a sign, foretaste, and instrument of God's victory over the power of sin and death. As the community under the sovereignty of Christ, the church is the body of Christ in the world—an extension of Christ's ministry.

The church's purpose is not its own. The church belongs to God and not to us. The church is to be present in the world on behalf of the God by whose grace it has been called into existence. What is the nature of God's presence in the world? God's presence is creative and redemptive. Where there is chaos, whether in the natural or social realm, God is present to create harmony. Where there is bondage—personal, political, or social—God is active to liberate and free the enslaved. Where there are walls dividing human beings into the privileged and the deprived, God seeks to destroy oppressive divisions through judgment and reconciliation. Where there is despair, loneliness, brokenness, and sickness, God is present to heal and mend. As Jesus Christ came "to bring good news to the poor, . . . to proclaim release to the captives and recovery of sight to the blind, to let the oppressed go free, to proclaim the year of the Lord's favor" (Luke 4:18), so the church is to be redemptively present with the poor, the captive, the blind, and the oppressed. It is to announce in word and deed the coming of God's justice and righteousness.

The church exists as an alternative community, a light to the world, a beacon of God's coming kingdom brought near in Jesus Christ. Its radical hospitality, which reaches beyond boundaries of race and class, points toward God's universal love. Its concern for and friendship with the impoverished, the despised, and vulnerable people of the world announces God's special presence with the marginalized, the abused, and the outcast. The church's moral integrity and commitment to justice is a prophetic witness to God's holiness and righteousness. Its generosity in responding to the needs of people around the world points toward God's self-giving abundance. The centrality of worship holds before the world the presence of transcendent beauty, goodness, truth, and love. A church shaped by divine grace stands as an alternative to society's reliance on success, prestige, wealth, and power as means of happiness and salvation.[7]

God's redemptive and creative presence is not limited to one denomination. Methodists are part of the church universal. In the Apostles' Creed, we affirm our belief in and commitment to "the holy catholic church," God's covenant community, which transcends national boundaries, denominational structures, and historical presence. We are part of God's universal and eternal presence and mission. As a member of the body of Christ, The United Methodist Church makes a distinctive contribution to God's universal and timeless mission.

The church is a means of grace, an embodiment of God's power to create, heal, forgive, reconcile, and transform the world. As a means of grace, the church is present in the world as an agent for inviting persons into relationship with Jesus Christ. The church works to form persons within the community in the likeness of Christ, and sends them forth into the world as agents of reconciliation and transformation. As the Body of the Risen Christ, the church points toward the kingdom of God, provides foretastes of God's coming reign, and works to accomplish God's purposes in the world.

Methodism's Distinctive Contributions

The United Methodist Church shares with the church universal a common faith in Jesus Christ. We share a common mission to be present in the world as God is present. United Methodism's structure and polity reflect three theological/missional emphases that contribute significantly to the universal church. These emphases are often interpreted administratively and bureaucratically rather than theologically and missionally. However, only by understanding the theological and missional foundation for connectionalism, itineracy, and catholicity can United Methodism live its identity and fulfill its mission.

CONNECTIONALISM

The United Methodist Church is a connectional church. Ever since John Wesley referred to Methodist classes, bands, and societies scattered throughout eighteenth-century England as "the connexion," the "people called Methodists" have understood themselves as a people of faith who journey together in covenant with God and one another. Our identity is in our wholeness together in Christ. Each part is vital to the whole. No local congregation, no conference or general church agency functions in isolation. Every aspect of the church's life functions in an intricate web of interdependency, support, and accountability.

Methodist connectionalism is rooted in the biblical concept of covenant. God entered into covenant with Abraham and Sarah and their descendants. They were to be God's people, a light to all nations. God would be their God and would lead them toward the fulfillment of the divine vision for humanity. As a covenant people, the people of Israel were to obey God's commands, practicing justice and mercy toward one another and all peoples. The twelve tribes of Israel were bound together by their covenant with God and with one another as the people of God.

The United Methodist Church is made up of local congregations, districts, annual conferences, jurisdictional conferences, and the general or global conference. Each component has authority and responsibility; each is related to, dependent upon, and in ministry with the other components. The covenant is expressed through shared missional efforts around the world, shared financial support, appointed pastoral leadership, oversight by bishops and district superintendents, a doctrinal statement, constitution, and structural polity approved by the General Conference. No one person or organization within The United Methodist Church is autonomous. Everyone and all structures are accountable to the whole, reminding us that the final authority is Christ.

Our connectionalism, then, is an expression of our understanding of the church as the body of Christ, with each part of the body having distinctive functions (1 Corinthians 12; Ephesians 4). Yet, each part is related to and dependent upon the others. Through our connectional relationships, we are reminded of our covenant with God, which transcends our differences and thereby enables us to maintain unity amid diversity. Through God's grace, we are connected with God's own life and we share in fellowship and ministry with diverse peoples throughout the world and throughout history.

Connectionalism is also a missional strategy. We can do together what no individual, congregation, or conference can do alone. Because of our connectional polity, The United Methodist Church provides a holistic ministry to the entire world. Through connectional channels, United Methodists have several hundred missionaries in countries throughout the world. Emergency and relief assistance is sent immediately into areas where disasters occur. Education is provided in scores of colleges and universities and seminaries. Curriculum and Bible study materials for all ages and settings are produced. Leadership training and resources are provided. Neighborhood centers, hospitals, retirement and nursing homes, childcare programs and institutions, and urban and rural mission centers minister to thousands of people in the name of Christ. As people in covenant with God and one another, The United Methodist Church seeks to embody the central affirmation expressed by the Apostle Paul: "In Christ, God was reconciling the world to himself . . . and entrusting the message of reconciliation to us" (2 Corinthians 5:19).

ITINERANCY

Itinerancy is another distinctive emphasis of Methodism. Clergy have their membership in the annual conference rather than the local church. Clergy are assigned to their areas of ministry by a bishop. Bishops are elected by the jurisdictional conferences and their membership is in the Council of Bishops. Bishops are assigned to conferences by the Jurisdictional Committee on the Episcopacy. All clergy, therefore, hold membership in a body to which they are accountable and they are appointed to their specific area of ministry. They are subject to assignment in accordance with the missional needs of the church.

Itinerancy is grounded in two basic theological affirmations: incarnation and a called and sent ministry. God's presence and truth have become incarnate in Jesus Christ. Jesus is the unique and supreme embodiment of the presence, love, and mission of the eternal God. However, God seeks to incarnate the divine presence, love, and mission in every person. Each person has unique gifts, qualities, and perspectives that God calls forth and uses as a means of ministry to the world. Since God's fullness has only been incarnate in one person—Jesus Christ—all others express only partial manifestations of God's presence and ministry. No pastor or layperson can adequately bear witness to the fullness of divine grace. Itinerant ministry affirms that each pastor brings unique gifts and perspectives, which over time provides congregations diverse ministers and, ideally, fuller expressions of God's presence and ministry.

John Wesley encountered objections to an itinerant ministry early in the formation of Methodism. Wesley followed the practice of moving preachers first every two years and then mostly every year. The rationale was rooted in Wesley's incarnational understanding of ministry. He wrote, "This [itinerancy] has always shown that the people profit less by any one person than by a variety of preachers; while they 'used the gifts on each bestowed, tempered by the act of God.'"[8] Wesley assigned preachers with the assumption that the people benefited from the variety of gifts that preachers bring to ministry.

Itinerancy has also functioned as a counter to preacher-worship. Methodists traditionally have avoided basing their loyalty to the church on a particular pastor. Pastors are temporary; our commitment is to Jesus Christ whose ministry transcends the personalities of the pastors. Since no one pastor embodies the fullness of God's grace and mission, the congregation can celebrate the gifts of each pastor and pastors can affirm the unique gifts and ministries of a variety of congregations.

The history of God's mission to the world has always included the calling and sending of people. Itinerancy affirms the called and sent nature of ministry. All ministry is participation in God's ministry to and with the world. Laity and clergy share in that called and sent ministry.

We are called to be the people of God and sent into the world to bear witness to God's grace-filled action on behalf of the world. Itinerancy reminds us, laity and clergy, that we are a pilgrim people who are called out (the *ecclesia*) and sent toward the new heaven and new earth, the kingdom of God. We are not homesteaders; we are sojourners, living temporarily in this world while our citizenship is in another world. We are always under command of Christ who called the disciples and sent them out to proclaim the coming of the kingdom. We are not our own; we have been called, empowered, and sent.

In addition to being an expression of incarnation and a called and sent ministry, itinerancy is also a missional strategy. John Wesley adopted an itinerant ministry as a means of deploying preachers where they were most needed. Called "traveling preachers," they were expected to move throughout the connection in order to evangelize. Circuit riders were deployed on the American frontier, often arriving in an area with or before the first homesteaders. The ability to deploy leadership quickly and strategically helps to account for the success of the Methodists in evangelization and the planting of new congregations across the American frontier.

Itinerancy has changed significantly since Wesley sent preachers across eighteenth-century England and into the prisons, slums, and open fields. Itinerancy is not the same today as when circuit riders rode into the wilderness of the new world. Longer tenure and consultation are necessary accommodations to the changing needs and dynamics of American culture. However, the theological and missional foundation of itinerancy remains a strong witness to the world, provided it is not eroded by a localism which compromises the broader mission and a clergy professionalism that uses itinerancy to enhance career advancement or promote personal agendas.

CATHOLICITY

Another distinctive ecclesial emphasis of Methodists is catholicity, or unity among God's people. Just as no local congregation or connectional component can be a full expression of the body of Christ, neither can one denomination. God's grace-filled ministry encompasses the full range of denominational structures and polities. Denominational chauvinism and competitiveness are contrary to the Wesleyan tradition. Openness to diversity, tolerance of differences, and ecumenical or cooperative ministries have characterized Methodism since its inception.

Methodism's historic ecumenical emphasis is expressed in Wesley's famous sermon entitled "Catholic Spirit." He wrote:

> I dare not therefore presume to impose my mode of worship on any other. I believe it is truly primitive and apostolical. But my belief is no rule for another. I ask not therefore of him with whom I would unite in love, "Are you of my Church? Of my congregation? Do you receive the same form of church government and allow the same church officers with me? Do you join in the same form of prayer wherein I worship God?" I inquire not, "Do you receive the Supper of the Lord in the same posture and manner that I do?" Nor whether, in the administration of baptism, you agree with me in admitting sureties for the baptized, in the manner of administering it, or the age of those to whom it should be administered . . . Let all these things stand by: we will talk of them, if need be, at a more convenient season. My only question at present is this, "Is thine heart right, as my heart is with thy heart?"[9]

Wesley affirmed that love for God and neighbor is the heart of religion and the catholic (universal) spirit is catholic (universal) love. The theme of General Conference in 1996 was *"In essentials, unity; in nonessentials, liberty; and in all things, charity."* The origin of the phrase is unknown, but it expresses an affirmation compatible with Methodism's long-standing commitment to sound doctrine, theological exploration, and the supremacy of love in all relationships. Though John Wesley never used the expression, he would have been sympathetic with the main point.[10]

Catholic spirit and tolerance of differences, however, are not to be interpreted as indifference to sound doctrine. Wesley warned:

> Observe this, you who know not what spirit ye are of, who call yourselves men of a catholic spirit only because you are of a muddy understanding; because your mind is all in a mist; because you have not settled, consistent principles, but are for jumbling all opinions together.[11]

Methodists, therefore, affirm the core doctrines of the apostolic faith. Beliefs and doctrines, however, are always subordinate to love for God and neighbor. Doctrinal differences can never be used as rationale for persecuting, hating, or failing to love another. Rather, United Methodist doctrines compel us to work for unity within the Christian church and embody Jesus' prayer: "I ask not only on behalf of these, but also on behalf of those who will believe in me through their word, that they may all be one. As you, Father, are in me and I am in you, may they also be in us, so that the world may believe that you sent me" (John 17:20-21).

As the Father, Son, and Holy Spirit are distinctive yet One, the church is called to exhibit to the world a unity that transcends all differences. In Christ, God has already broken down the dividing walls of hostility and made us one (Ephesians 2). Our catholicity as Methodists is a sign of the reconciliation wrought in Jesus Christ. A dominant biblical image of God's vision for the world is that the human family will be one; that people will come to know themselves as children of God and as brothers and sisters under the parenthood of God. The church is to be shaped by that vision of catholicity or unity. The United Methodist emphasis on catholic spirit summons all to live in union with one another under the sovereignty of God's universal love.

Conclusion

God's preoccupation is the salvation of the world, the reconciliation of all things in Jesus Christ. The church is called to share in God's ministry of salvation and reconciliation. The calling is fulfilled as the people of God live in accordance with God's revelation in Jesus Christ. The church is to embody the power, presence, and love of God, and to participate in the divine initiative to bring justice, peace, joy, and love to all creation. The church, therefore, is a sign that points to God's presence and purposes. It is a foretaste of God's coming victory already begun in the life, teaching, death, resurrection, and ascension of Jesus Christ. The church is to be an instrument that God uses to bring the kingdom of justice, generosity, and joy.

The church is our identity; it is not an organization to which we belong in accordance with our preferences and convenience. We are a called people, shaped and empowered by the Christ whom we serve.

As we live our identity in the home, the school, the neighborhood, the workplace, the political arena, and the institutional church, we share in God's life and mission. We become an alternative community bound together by common loyalty to Jesus Christ.

United Methodism is one manifestation of the universal church. Within the broader church, Methodists offer at least three distinctive ecclesial emphases: connectionalism, itineracy, and catholicity. The fragmented, broken world needs the witness of a community connected by a covenant with God and one another. A society that places priority on individualism and "doing my own thing" longs for models of servant leadership reflected in a sense of being called and sent to incarnate the grace of God. When religious differences continue to fuel animosity and violence, a church that emphasizes catholicity or universal love is essential. The contemporary world needs the witness of The United Methodist Church.

Opportunities for Reflection

The following questions may be used by groups wishing to discuss the material in chapter nine or by individuals wanting to reflect on issues raised within the chapter.

1. Methodism began as a renewal movement within the Anglican Church and Wesley said that God had raised up the Methodists "to reform the nation, particularly the Church, and to spread scriptural holiness over the land." In what ways is The United Methodist Church today fulfilling and/or failing to fulfill its original mission? Discuss the current statement of the church's mission ("to make disciples of Jesus Christ for the transformation of the world") in light of the mission "to reform the nation, particularly the Church, and to spread scriptural holiness."

2. Where have you experienced the church as "a means of grace" in your own life? Share an experience in which the church has been a vehicle of God's presence and power to heal, forgive, reconcile, and transform.

3. What do you consider as distinctive contributions The United Methodist Church makes to the broader Christian witness today? What do United Methodists share in common with other Christian denominations? In what ways does the existence of several denominations strengthen and/or weaken the unity of the body of Christ?

4. How does your local congregation view connectionalism, itinerancy, and catholic spirit? What changes do you suggest for strengthening the connection, itinerancy, and unity?

5. Methodism began as a reform and missional movement. In what ways might United Methodism continue its historic work?

6. What strengths does connectionalism offer the world? What strengths does catholicity offer? Itinerancy?

10

Doctrinal Faithfulness and Continuing Exploration

Sharing God's life and mission involves us in an endless journey and continuous growth in understanding. Since God is more than can be totally described in creeds or comprehended by human minds, relationship with God and participating in God's mission require continuing exploration and persistent openness to new insights and revelations. God's reconciled and redeemed creation is only partially realized in human history. Therefore, participating in the divine mission requires an unending effort to discern God's vision and a willingness to follow Christ in the power of the Holy Spirit into new arenas of service. Every age presents the people of God with new challenges and new frontiers of mission. Apostolic faith and mission must be interpreted and applied anew in every generation and each new context.

The contemporary world presents the Christian faith with particular challenges. The world of the twenty-first century is vastly different from the age of the apostles or the era of John Wesley. Science and technology have altered every aspect of life—our food, clothing, shelter, transportation, communication, medicine, education, entertainment, work, and worldview. Life and death decisions, once attributed only to God, are now thrust upon us. Places and people—once so distant as to remain unknown—are now within easy reach by telephone, television, email, and travel. We once could choose to ignore people in distant lands with different religious traditions and varied political and economic systems. However, those diverse people are now our neighbors in this global village. Information, once inaccessible to the masses or stored in books, is now instantaneously and conveniently accessible through home computers and compact cell phones/computers. Feats that at one time were considered fictional or miraculous are performed daily in hospitals, airports and space launching pads, scientific laboratories, and manufacturing facilities.

Is God a stranger in this new world of science and technology and cultural and religious pluralism? Is God's presence limited only to those who know and affirm the Christian creeds? Or, one youth asked, "Does God understand nuclear physics and genetics?" The world of space exploration, gene manipulation, computer technology, organ transplants, test-tube babies, economic interdependency, and global neighborhoods challenges traditional concepts of God and God's relationship with the world. Without a willingness to engage in serious explorations into God's nature, purpose, and presence, the church will answer questions nobody is asking and become a mere monument to a static and absent God.

Methodism affirms the necessity of maintaining the truth of historic apostolic doctrines and engaging in continuing explorations into God's life and mission. The tension between holding fast the doctrines and interpreting and applying ancient revelation to new situations is the growing edge of faith and obedience. Sharing the life of a God who is sovereign of the past, present, and future demands loyalty to what God has done and openness to what God is doing and shall do.

Exploring New Frontiers of Faith

Remaining faithful to the apostolic faith, while interpreting and applying that faith to contemporary situations, is the task of every Christian. The temptation is to remove the inherent tension of faith by opting for either dogmatic creedalism or doctrinal indifferentism. Both rigid dogma and indifference to sound doctrine are contrary to United Methodist tradition and practice. *The Book of Discipline* describes the role of doctrine and theological reflection:

> While the Church considers its doctrinal affirmations as a central feature of its identity and restricts official changes to a constitutional process, the Church encourages serious reflection across the theological spectrum.
>
> As United Methodists, we are called to identify the needs both of individuals and of society and to address those needs out of the resources of Christian faith in a way that is clear, convincing, and effective. Theology serves the Church by interpreting the world's needs and challenges to the Church and by interpreting the gospel to the world.[1]

By placing emphasis upon both doctrine and continuing theological exploration, United Methodists acknowledge that faith is dynamic, growing, and relevant to changing contexts. Sharing in God's life and participating in God's mission is more than mental assent to ancient creeds. It is an endless process of understanding what God has done, discerning what God is doing, envisioning what God will do, and giving oneself to God's mission. Faith is acting upon the truth God has revealed and is revealing and remaining faithful even when God seems incomprehensible, remote, or absent. Faithfulness involves trusting and remaining committed to the God made known in Jesus Christ even though the changing world raises questions and presents new challenges to our faith.

The historic doctrines of the church provide a place to stand amid the shifting sands of turbulent change. These doctrines are lenses through which to view competing faith claims. They also serve as home base from which we launch continuing explorations into God's being and mission. Without historic doctrines, our explorations are without compass and guide. The results are needless wanderings in the wilderness of confusion, being led astray by destructive idols, and distorting God's nature and mission.

Doctrines provide a framework and parameters for understanding God and exploring God's nature and purpose. Dr. Thomas Langford suggests a helpful analogy: "Doctrine is like a house that a religious communion already inhabits. It represents a communal agreement about what is essential to and characteristic of their faith."[2] Theological inquiry, on the other hand, "is the proposal of blueprints for extending the house. Often individually drawn, these blueprints represent creative efforts to suggest new construction which will make the home more welcoming or adequate."[3]

Living in the house of faith and engaging in new construction require the use of reliable tools. Doctrine as stated in the historic creeds, Articles of Religion, and Confession of Faith represent the basic blueprints that have to be constantly interpreted and to which expansions or "change orders" must cohere. The following are the tools affirmed by The United Methodist Church as necessary and reliable tools for maintaining sound doctrine and engaging in theological reflection and exploration:[4]

- scripture;
- tradition;
- experience; and
- reason.

THE CENTRALITY OF THE BIBLE

The primary source and criterion for determining doctrine and engaging in theological exploration is the Bible. The centrality of scripture in matters of faith is clearly declared in the United Methodist standards of doctrine. The Articles of Religion include the following:

> The Holy Scriptures containeth all things necessary to salvation; so that whatsoever is not read therein, nor may be proved thereby, is not to be required of any man that it should be believed as an article of faith, or be thought requisite or necessary to salvation.[5]

As stated in a previous chapter, John Wesley referred to himself as "a man of one book." He wrote, "I began not only to read, but to study the Bible, as the one, the only standard of truth, and the only model of pure religion."[6] Albert Outler writes, "Wesley's point of departure was always Holy Scripture, understood according to the 'analogy of faith' (i.e., its general sense), and as 'the standing revelation' in the Christian Church throughout her long history."[7]

United Methodists believe that the Bible is primary in matters of faith and its authority lies in the Living Word to which the Bible bears witness. It is not the verbal inspiration or factual accuracy that gives the Bible authority. God's revelation, supremely given in Christ, is the Bible's source of authority. The Bible serves for us the role that John the Baptist served for the Messiah. He bore witness to the Light but was not to be equated with the Light. The Bible points to the One who is life's supreme authority, the Triune God who was incarnate in Jesus Christ.

United Methodists take the Bible with utmost seriousness even though many do not take it literally. Serious reading of the Bible requires taking its historical and literary setting into consideration. It involves entering the world of the Bible, struggling with its language and symbols, literary devices, and cultural context. Taking the Bible seriously requires that the reader be open to the Holy Spirit who brings the Eternal Word into the midst of the temporal needs of the reader. Reading the Bible in solitude and in community is a means of understanding God and sharing in God's guiding and empowering presence in the contemporary contexts.

The Bible, of course, can be misused. Although the Bible is considered as the primary source and criterion for understanding God's revelation, its truths and insights are not self-evident. Scripture does not yield its divine secrets carelessly or casually. Discerning the Eternal Word within the words of the Bible demands hard work and risky struggle. Most Christians need help in using the Bible as a vehicle of God's presence and revelation. Following are a few general guidelines for interpreting scripture.[8]

First, the Bible is to be read and studied primarily as the story about God and God's relationship with creation and human beings. Although it contains history, science, psychology, and various types of literature, the Bible is principally a book of *theology*, the story of God. It is not meant to be a textbook of science or history. History is recounted not primarily to provide facts about events but to reveal something about God. Facts and details are less important than the deeper truth of God's presence and purposes. For example, the story of Jonah in the Old Testament does not focus on a fish swallowing a man. Its central revelation is this: God's mercy and love are universal and includes those we may label as enemies. The creation stories in Genesis are not scientific accounts of how creation came into being. They are affirmations that creation and human beings have their origin and existence in God who brings order out of chaos, light out of darkness, life out of nothingness.

Second, each part of the Bible is to be interpreted in terms of the total message of scripture. Reading passages in isolation from the broader biblical message results in proof-texting and may distort God's revelation. All passages must be interpreted in the light of the life, teachings, death, and resurrection of Jesus Christ. That is, Jesus Christ is the measure of the Bible's message. That which contradicts the spirit of Jesus must be treated with suspicion or subordination. For example, a passage such as Psalm 137:9 that extols the slaughter of the enemy's children must be read in its context and measured against Jesus' treatment of children and his warning to those who would harm them.

Third, each book of the Bible must be interpreted first in terms of its historical context. When was it written? Who wrote it? What was the situation the book sought to address? What did it mean to the persons to whom it was written? In order to know what the Bible *means*, we must know what it *meant*. Severing scripture from its historical context results in manipulating its message to serve the interpreter's purposes. Failing to understand, for example, that the Book of Revelation was written to give encouragement to people being persecuted at the hands of the Roman emperor can lead to misusing the book to frighten the faithful or to foretell future events.

Fourth, each passage is to be read and interpreted in its literary context. Where is the passage located? What precedes and follows it in the text? What kind of literature is it? Poetry? Prose? Narrative? Letter? Parable? Allegory? Prophecy? Apocalypse? What literary devices are used? Understanding the literary form and context enables the reader to get inside the biblical material and sense its drama and insight. One can identify with the characters in the stories, experience the surroundings, feel the movement, and confront the issues. Reading the Psalms as prayers and hymns, for example, can give expression to our own feelings and needs in the presence of God.

Fifth, after considering the passage in its broader biblical, historical, and literary context, the interpreter begins to raise questions as to the implications for his or her own life and experience. Where am I in the story? What are the similarities between the situation addressed in the passage and our own situation? What are the differences? What does the passage say about God, God's presence, or God's purposes in and for our time and my life? What difference would it make if we lived in terms of this passage? What changes would take place? What are the obstacles to living in terms of this passage? Does the Bible offer insight and motivation for removing the obstacles? Can I illustrate the insight of this passage in my own life?

Sixth, the reader may wish to consult what others have said or written about the passage. Numerous commentaries are available that help one understand the historical and literary context and to provide insights others have gleaned from the passage. *The Wesley Study Bible* (Abingdon Press) and *The Meeting God Bible* (Upper Room Books) are both valuable resources for personal study. Sharing insights from and with the church's biblical scholars and students is a means of being held accountable and it makes one less likely to misinterpret and misuse the Bible. Also, reading the Bible devotionally with the aid of such resources as *The Upper Room Daily Devotional* and lectionary studies can be helpful and illuminating.

Seventh, the Bible is to be studied in community with other Christians. The Bible was written by a community, within a community, and for the community. It has been preserved and interpreted across the centuries by an expansive and diverse community. We are surrounded by "a great cloud of witnesses" as we search the scriptures for understanding God's nature and mission. As the Christian community's book, the Bible is to be read and studied in community. Being part of a Bible study group is important and vital, as many who have participated in *Disciple Bible Study* have found.[9]

TRADITION AS A SOURCE AND TOOL FOR KNOWING AND SERVING GOD

While the Bible is the primary and central tool for interpreting the blueprints of the house of faith and determining expansions and renovations, tradition plays a vital role in clarifying doctrine and engaging in theological exploration. *The Book of Discipline* states:

> The theological task does not start anew in each age or each person. Christianity does not leap from New Testament times to the present as though nothing were to be learned from that great cloud of witnesses in between. For centuries Christians have sought to interpret the truth of the gospel for their time.[10]

According to the Bible, God speaks and acts in the events of history. The Exodus of the Hebrews from Egyptian slavery, the giving of the Law on Sinai, the building of the Hebrew nation, the Assyrian and Babylonian captivity and subsequent restoration, the Incarnation in Jesus of Nazareth, Pentecost, and the creation of the church—these are foundational events in the church's history. The hymns, prayers, teachings, stories, and liturgies of Judaism and the early church form part of the storehouse of the church's tradition. The writings of the early church leaders contain revelatory insights that cannot be ignored by those who seek to know God in the contemporary world. Neither can we ignore the historic creeds and the life stories of pilgrims of faith through the ages. The historic church councils confronted issues and questions that continue to have relevance for understanding who God is and what God desires for the world. The cumulative experience of our mothers and fathers in the faith form the story that gives us identity and vision for the future.

Tradition is multifaceted and diverse. Our tradition includes stories of the church's misunderstanding of God and distortions of the church's mission. We must learn from the failures and avoid repeating them. The tradition, therefore, must be interpreted holistically and in the light of scripture. Tradition can be used to justify actions and beliefs that are contrary to scripture and the example and spirit of Jesus. Nevertheless, tradition reflects a continuity of experience and revelation. Ignoring the continuity of tradition's themes and insights in our continuing quest is as absurd as attempting to face each new day with no memory of the past.

John Wesley urged his contemporaries to "acquire a 'knowledge of the Fathers,'" because they were the most authentic commentators on scripture, as being both nearest to the fountain, and eminently endued with that Spirit by whom all scripture is given.[11] Wesley was as familiar with the early history of the church as any person in eighteenth-century England. He could readily call upon the thinking, insights, and experiences of the early church fathers and mothers and the broader church tradition as a resource for confronting issues of life and faith. Few United Methodists today, however, are adequately acquainted with church traditions, often assuming that the new is more authoritative and relevant than the old. The historic creeds—such as the Apostles' Creed, the Nicene Creed, and the Articles of Religion and Confession of Faith in our own *Book of Discipline*—along with the hymns and liturgies of the church provide concise summaries and dominant themes of traditional theological insights and parameters. The church's history contains a wellspring of God's revelation that can guide us in exploring contemporary challenges and opportunities.

Tradition also includes the broader range of human experience. Just as God acts uniquely in each person, so God acts uniquely in each culture. Therefore, learning and appreciating the traditions of other cultures can be a means of deepening our understanding and experience of God. African-Americans, Hispanics, Africans, Asians, Native Americans, Latinos, as well as Europeans comprise the traditions of Methodism. Included in our doctrinal and liturgical heritage are pietism, evangelicalism, revivalism, social action, high liturgy, and liturgical spontaneity. All contribute to the ongoing journey toward the fullness of God's presence and revelation.

EXPERIENCE AS A SOURCE AND TOOL FOR KNOWING AND SERVING GOD

Experience is both an avenue of God's presence and a tool for discerning God's purposes. Grace, God's presence and power, is mediated in and through the experiences of living. There is a transcendent dimension to all experiences as the Holy Spirit works within life's joys and sorrows, successes and failures, hopes and disappointments, challenges and conflicts, solitariness and relationships. Growth in understanding and trusting God and faithfulness in discipleship involve persistently scanning the depths of our experiences for signs of the presence and guidance of the One in whom "we live and move and have our being" (Acts 17:28).

The Wesleyan understanding of experience is twofold. First and foremost, it refers to the personal experience of God's convicting, justifying, pardoning, and reconciling grace. It is experiencing the need for repentance, knowing the assurance of forgiveness, and growing in love for God and neighbor. *The Book of Discipline* explains it this way: "'New life in Christ' is what we as United Methodists mean when we speak of 'Christian experience.'"[12] All doctrines and theological reflections, according to Methodist tradition, have as their basic purpose and authority the experience of God's prevenient, justifying, and sanctifying grace. A valid question to ask of all doctrines and beliefs is this: Does it promote or enhance new life in Christ?

Experience in the Wesleyan understanding also refers to the common-sense experience of the individual and the community. Experiences of the individual and the entire human family are avenues of insight and revelation, as well as criteria by which beliefs are judged. Our life experiences influence how we perceive God, how we come to know God, and how we express our loyalty to God. The Methodist emphasis on practical divinity leads us to ask of all theological affirmations, "Does it ring true in my experience and in the experience of the Christian community?" If it does, experience has helped to validate the affirmation. If it is incompatible with our experience, the belief may either be a challenge to our experience or the experience may be a challenge to the validity of the belief.

Experience, too, can be misleading and must be tested by scripture, tradition, and reason within the context of Christian community. My personal feelings and experiences are not the final authority when it comes to valid doctrine or faithful theological reflection. My feelings and experiences must be held up against the blueprint of scripture, located within the experience of the church throughout history, and subjected to the critique of reason. Apart from Christian community grounded in scripture and connected to tradition, spiritual gratification and private subjective feelings are elevated as primary religious experiences. Psychology verifies that self-interpretations of our experience can be gross distortions of reality. Methodists, therefore, do not support the popular notion of "being spiritual without the church." Christian experience is formed and nurtured in practices that open us to God's presence and power, such as the General Rules as discussed in chapter eight. Our own personal experiences require the broader experiences of others to inform, correct, and support us if we are to know the fullness of divine grace.

REASON AS A SOURCE AND TOOL FOR KNOWING AND SERVING GOD

Jesus said that the entire law is summed up in this commandment: "You shall love the Lord your God with all your heart, and with all your soul, and with all your mind, and with all your strength" (Mark 12:30). The human mind is one of God's most precious gifts and an important means of exploring, discerning, and sharing God's truth and mission. *The Book of Discipline* contains the following statement:

> Since all truth is from God, efforts to discern the connections between revelation and reason, faith and science, grace and nature, are useful endeavors in developing credible and communicable doctrine. We seek nothing less than a total view of reality that is decisively informed by the promises and imperatives of the Christian gospel.[13]

The following is John Wesley's response in 1768 to a Cambridge professor who accused the Methodists of renouncing reason: "It is a fundamental principle with us that to renounce reason is to renounce religion; that religion and reason go hand and hand; and that all irrational religion is false religion."[14] Anti-intellectualism emerged among some Methodists on the American frontier and residues of it continue into the twenty-first century. However, any attempt to denigrate reason must be resisted if United Methodists are to be true to their heritage and if they are to be a compelling voice in the contemporary world where the scientific method dominates intellectual circles.

The issues confronting the church and the broader world community are enormously complex. Developments in science and technology have raised new ethical dilemmas and challenges to conventional theological thinking. Discoveries in genetics, for example, have reopened the debates about determinism and freedom of the will, as well as the definition of human life. Global warming and climate change require revisiting the meaning of creation as God's gift and dominion as a prerogative of human beings. Medical breakthroughs force us to deal with questions about the initiation and termination of life.

Bearing witness to the Christian gospel in such a world requires both a tough mind and a compassionate heart. How are we to know the mind of Christ on such issues as genetic engineering, human sexuality, abortion, environmental policy, war, international conflict, and the growing gap between the economically rich and the poor? How are we to understand the Christian gospel in relationship to Judaism, Islam, Hinduism, and other religions? What do we have to say to those whose intellectual worldview does not include God?

These are but a few of the questions and challenges that highlight the necessity of reason as a vital tool in understanding and interpreting God's nature and mission. Methodism has a long tradition of involvement in education as testimony to our conviction that we are to love God with the mind and to responsibly employ reason as integral to faithful discipleship.

Although an important tool for doctrine and theological exploration, reason has its limitations. Like all other gifts and resources made available for sharing God's life and mission, reason can be misdirected and abused. A misshaped mind is a dangerous thing! The intellect can be, and often is, used as a tool for diabolical evil and cataclysmic devastation. The terrible atrocities of Nazism, for example, were conceived and implemented by highly intelligent, well-educated people. Intelligence without character is perilous. Christian character is grounded in scripture, connected to and informed by tradition, and shaped by experiences born in and permeated by grace present in community. The charge by Jesus to the early apostles captures the appropriate role of reason in faithful discipleship and mission: "See, I am sending you out like sheep into the midst of wolves: so be wise as serpents and innocent as doves" (Matthew 10:16). The astute mind and the grace-formed character are indispensable tools for knowing and serving God in the present age.

Scripture, tradition, reason, and experience provide Methodists with resources and guidelines for their endless journey into God's life and mission. When used as interrelated and mutually dependent tools, they enable persons of faith to grow in discipleship as they confront the challenges of living in the modern world. *The Book of Discipline* states, "These four sources—each making distinctive contributions, yet all finally working together—guide our quest as United Methodists for a vital and appropriate Christian witness."[15]

Conclusion

We live in a world that is increasingly indifferent or even hostile to Christian beliefs and practices. Even the most faithful disciples of Jesus Christ are challenged to rethink their faith in the face of changing concepts and demands. Living our faith in a personal God in an impersonal world and infinite universe is not easy. Trusting in the power of Transcendent Love in a society that relies on weapons of war, technological skill, and economic security presents us with a formidable challenge. A world filled with suffering, violence, poverty, and needless death raises questions about the existence of One who is both loving and powerful. Indeed, the journey of faith in the twenty-first century takes the faithful through new theological territory.

Yet, we are not left without resources in our journey. The God whom we follow into the future is present to guide, sustain, and shape us as individuals and as a church. We enter the new territory with memory and hope. The historic doctrines of the Christian faith provide a framework within which we can explore the new territory. Through serious study of the Bible, the God who in Jesus Christ has made all things new continues to reveal the eternal and transcendent presence and purposes. From the tradition of the church in all its diversity, we are surrounded by a great cloud of witnesses who have followed the footsteps of God into new territory. Within the human mind and experience, the Holy Spirit is present to illumine, question, inform, and bring pardon and new life.

We, therefore, enter the future with confidence that the God who is sovereign of the past, present, and future will meet us in the challenges, dangers, uncertainties, and opportunities that await us in the perilous and promising future.

Opportunities for Reflection

The following questions may be used by groups wishing to discuss the material in chapter ten or by individuals wanting to reflect on issues raised within the chapter.

1. How would you explain the difference between doctrine and theological exploration? What role do the historic creeds play in your own understanding of God's nature and mission? One scholar has described the affirmations of faith as more "pledges of allegiance" than mere summaries of intellectual affirmations.[16] What does it mean to affirm the Apostles' Creed in worship?

2. What role does the Bible play in your own relationship with God? What is the difference, if any, in taking the Bible literally and taking it seriously? What is your response to the point that the Bible is authoritative in matters of faith but is not a book primarily of science or history? Select a passage from the Bible and use the seven guidelines identified in this chapter to study and reflect on the passage.

3. What is your response to the Wesleyan understanding of experience? Share an experience in which you have known God's grace personally?

4. How important is reason in your own faith journey? What are the theological puzzles or vexing issues that you find difficult to think through in light of the Christian faith?

5. Select one of the issues or challenges confronting the church and world and discuss it in the light of the four sources and tools discussed in this chapter.

11

A New Heaven and a New Earth

A local station televised a documentary on homeless people in Knoxville, Tennessee. One of those interviewed, "Chief," lived in a makeshift tent on the bank of the Tennessee River. Though homeless and addicted to alcohol, Chief was intelligent, sensitive, and compassionate. He could converse with University of Tennessee students and faculty about philosophy and politics as easily as he could discuss survival skills with street peers. He often visited the soup kitchen at the local United Methodist Church, where he engaged the pastors in theological discussions. The televised documentary closed with a camera shot of Chief, returning along the river to his crude shelter. Shaking his head from side to side, Chief was saying, "The world ain't supposed to be like this."

Needless suffering and premature death, violence and cruelty, economic and political exploitation, adverse poverty and environmental destruction ravage the earth. Sin and death, guilt and grief, loneliness and fear, anxiety and alienation continue to rob the human family of abundant life. Wars rage among nations. Racial and religious prejudices erupt into violent hatred, mocking the biblical vision of peace and the oneness of the human family. We know "the world ain't supposed to be like this."

John Wesley observed that "darkness, intellectual darkness, ignorance, with vice and misery attendant upon it, cover the earth!"[1] The pervasive evil in the world raised for Wesley a critical theological question: "But how astonishing is this, if there is a God in heaven! And if his eyes are over all the earth! Can he despise the work of his own hand? . . . How is it possible to reconcile this with either the wisdom or goodness of God?"[2] The only satisfactory explanation, according to Wesley, is that the present condition of the world is not the final reality. God is bringing a new heaven and a new earth. The world is not what it is going to be! God's grace will prevail and transform the whole creation!

Along with other Christians, United Methodists look toward the consummation of God's purposes and the world will be as God intends. *The Book of Discipline* affirms, "We also look to the end time in which God's work will be fulfilled. This prospect gives us hope in our present actions, as individuals and as the Church. This expectation saves us from resignation and motivates our continuing witness and service."[3] We are a people who live toward the coming of God's new heaven and new earth.

The Future Revealed in Jesus Christ

The Apostle Paul described Jesus Christ as "the image of the invisible God, the firstborn of all creation . . . he is the beginning, the firstborn from the dead, so that he might come to have first place in everything. For in him all the fullness of God was pleased to dwell, and through him God was pleased to reconcile to himself all things, whether on earth or in heaven . . ." (Colossians 1:15,18-20). In Jesus Christ the new heaven and new earth is brought near. Through Jesus Christ in the power of the Holy Spirit, the reign of God's righteousness will be brought to completion.

The kingdom of God is the central theme of Jesus' teaching in the Synoptic Gospels. Mark's Gospel describes the beginning of Jesus' ministry in these words: "Now after John was arrested, Jesus came to Galilee, proclaiming the good news of God, and saying, 'The time is fulfilled, and the kingdom of God has come near; repent and believe in the good news'" (Mark 1:14-15). In Jesus, the reign of God—the power, presence, and purposes of God—comes near. Jesus Christ is the fulfillment of God's purposes. He is the manifestation of God's power and presence. His teachings and actions point to the reign of God. His death and resurrection proclaim the victory of God. His ascension affirms the promise of God.

In Jesus Christ, God manifests and inaugurates the new heaven and new earth through the Word-Made-Flesh, Jesus Christ. As the Gospel writer affirms: "All things came into being . . . and without him not one thing came into being" (John 1:3). From the very beginning, the Triune God has been conquering the powers of chaos, sin, and death, and establishing the reign of righteousness and love.

As "the firstborn of the new creation," Jesus Christ makes visible God's salvation of the whole creation—redeeming the past, renewing the present, and transforming the future. Jesus Christ is the image of existence as God intends, the Savior and Redeemer of the old world, and the assurance of the final triumph of God's new world. Through the life, teachings, death, and resurrection of Jesus Christ, God's reign over creation and God's triumph over the powers of sin and death are brought near and secured. God's new heaven and new earth have begun and will be brought to completion.

God's future is forever breaking in upon the present as a sign and foretaste of God's ultimate triumph over chaos, sin, and death. Wherever the will of God is done, the kingdom of God is present. God's reign comes near whenever love triumphs over hate, justice reigns over injustice, the shackles of oppression and addiction are removed, reconciliation overcomes alienation, hope drives out despair, and wholeness and health are restored to creation. Everywhere Jesus went he brought love, forgiveness, hope, healing, insight, life, and judgment. His very presence judged those in whom hatred, vengeance, despair, injustice, oppression, sin, and death reigned. Christ's invitation was and is,

"Come. Let us live in a new world, the world of God's sovereignty over life and death." Live now in the light of God's victory.

God's Final Victory Yet to Come

"Christ has died; Christ is risen; Christ will come again," we affirm in the Prayer of Great Thanksgiving.[4] The historic creeds of the church include belief in "the resurrection of the dead and the life in the world to come" (The Nicene Creed), in "the resurrection of the body and the life everlasting" (The Apostles' Creed), and "in the final triumph of righteousness and in life everlasting" (The Statement of Faith of the Korean Methodist Church).[5] From New Testament times to the present, the church has awaited the return of Christ, or the End. Eschatology—having to do with last things—has been a significant emphasis in the church's preaching and teachings. However, the theme has received less emphasis in the preaching and teaching of more recent United Methodists.

As a youngster, I heard many sermons on the end of time, the Second Coming, and the Final Judgment. Using the apocalyptic passages in the Bible (passages describing the End, including the books of Daniel and Revelation), preachers graphically portrayed the End of all things and the Second Coming of Christ, and the Final Judgment. They pointed to signs in the contemporary world that biblical prophecy was being fulfilled. Images of "weeping, wailing, and gnashing of teeth," "hellfire and brimstone," and the everlasting punishment of sinners summoned listeners to repent as the only appropriate preparation for the coming Judgment. I spent many sleepless nights afraid the end of the world would come "like a thief in the night." I feared I would be sent to hell, to burn forever. I was afraid that Christ would return and take my parents to heaven in "the rapture," leaving me to suffer tribulation and punishment.

This distorted apocalyptic emphasis on "the rapture" and "End Times" continues in the popular fictional *Left Behind* series by Tim LaHaye and Jerry Jenkins, as well as in the preaching of some segments of the church. The portrayal of contemporary events as the "fulfillment of biblical prophecy" and immutable signs that the End is drawing near

severs apocalyptic literature such as Revelation and Daniel from its historical context and subverts its message of hope and promise.

A respected United Methodist New Testament scholar, Craig C.
Hill, has written a helpful book on how Christians can interpret biblical
eschatology. After dealing with the popular portrayals by such expo-
nents as Hal Lindsey, Tim LaHaye, Jerry Jenkins, Kenneth Copeland,
Rex Humbard, John Hagee, and others, Dr. Hill writes:

> In sum, contemporary America's most popular Christian eschatol-
> ogy is unscriptural. Ironically, in their effort to interpret the Bible
> literally and consistently, proponents of the rapture have mangled
> the biblical witness almost beyond recognition. At the end of all
> their theorizing and systematizing, it is the Bible itself, this won-
> derfully diverse and complex witness to God and Christ, that has
> been left behind.[6]

Although the End or Second Coming (a term not used in the Bible)
includes judgment upon and the destruction of evil, God's final victory
brings hope, not despair. The Revelation to John, with its images of
celestial conflict between God and the forces of evil, is supremely a
book of hope and assurance rooted in God's triumph. The book was
written as a source of encouragement and strength in a time of cruel
persecution of Christians by the Roman emperor Nero or Domitian. It
is a ringing affirmation that the new heaven and new earth, inaugurated
in Jesus Christ, will be brought to completion. Here is the writer's partial description of God's new creation:

> Then I saw a new heaven and a new earth; for the first heaven and
> the first earth had passed away, and the sea was no more. And I
> saw the holy city, the new Jerusalem, coming down out of heaven
> from God, prepared as a bride adorned for her husband.
>
> And I heard a loud voice from the throne saying,
>
> "See, the home of God is among mortals.
> He will dwell with them as their God;
> they will be his peoples, and God himself will be with them;
> he will wipe every tear from their eyes.
> Death will be no more;
> mourning and crying and pain will be no more,
> for the first things have passed away."

And the one who was seated on the throne said, "See, I am making all things new." Also, he said, "Write this, for these words are
trustworthy and true." Then he said to me, "It is done! I am the
Alpha and the Omega, the beginning and the end. To the thirsty I
will give water as a gift from the spring of the water of life. Those
who conquer will inherit these things, and I will be their God and
they will be my children." (Revelation 21:1-8)

Belief in the Second Coming means that the victory begun in Jesus
Christ will be brought to completion. God will win! Evil will be con-
quered! God's purpose for the world will be fulfilled:

- Creation will be healed and Eden restored.
- Righteousness and peace will prevail and "they shall beat
  their swords into plowshares, and their spears into pruning
  hooks; nation shall not lift up sword against nation, neither
  shall they learn war any more" (Isaiah 2:4).
- People will know themselves as beloved children of God, and
  will be valued for their identity as sons and daughters of God.
- Barriers among people will be removed and the human fam-
  ily will be one.
- The presence and power of God will cover the earth as waters
  cover the sea.
- Death, pain, and sorrow will pass away.
- The lowly will be exalted, the last will be first, the weak will
  be made strong.
- The kingdoms of this world will become the kingdom of
  Christ.
- Christ shall reign forever!

John Wesley assured the early Methodists that God's reign will
come to completion. To the poor and despised, the discouraged, and
defeated of his day, he proclaimed:

We have strong reason to hope that the work he hath begun will
carry on unto the day of his Lord Jesus; that he will never intermit
this blessed work of his Spirit until he has fulfilled all his promises; until he hath put a period to sin and misery, and infirmity,
and death; and re-established universal holiness and happiness,
and caused all the inhabitants of the earth to sing together,

"Hallelujah! The Lord God omnipotent reigneth!" Blessing, and glory, and wisdom, and honour, and power, and might be unto our Lord God forever and ever![7]

Today's United Methodists live toward God's final victory. We believe that the salvation God has begun in us and that all creation will be brought to completion. Through the work of the Holy Spirit, we will be transformed into the likeness of Jesus Christ and incorporated into Christ's reign over death and sin. Although death brings grief and loss, we live with hope in life eternal and in the assurance that "neither death, nor life, nor angels, nor rulers, nor things present, nor things to come, nor powers, nor height, nor depth, nor anything else in all creation, will be able to separate us from the love of God in Christ Jesus our Lord" (Romans 8:38-39).

GOD'S VICTORY INCLUDES ALL CREATION

More than human life is to be transformed by God's final victory. All creation will be healed, from the scarred majestic mountains to the polluted flowing streams, from the depleted ozone to the microscopic cell, from the diseased mighty oak to the endangered spotted owl. The founder of Methodism captured the pervasiveness of God's cosmic triumph in these words:

> He that sitteth upon the throne will soon change the face of all things, and give a demonstrative proof to all his creatures that "his mercy is over all his works." The horrid state of things which at present obtains, will soon be at an end. On the new earth no creature will kill, or hurt, or give pain to any other. . . . Nay, no creature, no beast, bird, or fish, will have any inclination to hurt any other. For cruelty will be far away, and savageness and fierce ness be forgotten. So that violence shall be heard no more, neither wasting or destruction seen on the face of the earth. "The wolf shall dwell with the lamb . . . and the leopard shall lie down with the kid: They shall not hurt or destroy," from the rising of the sun to the going down of the same.[8]

God's Kingdom includes sovereignty over more than the human spirit and belief in God's final victory includes more than confidence in personal life after death, though we strongly affirm life after death. Christ is sovereign over all creation "and through him God was pleased to reconcile to himself all things, whether on earth or in heaven . . ." (Colossians 1:20). As Jesus calmed the stormy sea (Matthew 8:23-27), cast out demons (Mark 1:21-28), and raised Lazarus from the dead (John 11:28-44), so the Risen and Ascended Christ will heal all creation, conquer all demonic principalities and powers, and bring new life to humanity.

Because United Methodists affirm that God's sovereignty and salvation encompass the whole creation, the widespread notion that there is a dichotomy between "the personal gospel" and "the social gospel" runs contrary to our Wesleyan tradition. God's grace is universally present in the created order; that is, God's presence and power to create, heal, reconcile, and transform includes every dimension of existence—personal, social, political, economic, and physical as well as spiritual. There is one gospel with personal and social dimensions because God's grace-filled sovereignty is over all creation!

As we stated in the last chapter, "The church exists as an alternative community, a light to the world, a beacon of God's coming kingdom brought near in Jesus Christ." The church, therefore, is called to be a visible sign of God's present and coming reign in Jesus Christ and an instrument of God's grace and salvation. Consequently, the church is concerned about all that thwarts the coming of God's final victory—political corruption and oppression, economic injustices, racial and gender inequalities, diseases and needless suffering, premature death, and environmental exploitation and destruction.

LIVING NOW TOWARD GOD'S FINAL VICTORY

What does it mean to live our belief in God's final victory? It means to live now in the light of God's coming triumph. We are called, individually and as a church, to live today in terms of Christ's sovereignty over all creation. Belief in life after death and in the consummation of God's purposes revealed in Jesus Christ involves more than anticipation of the future. It means incorporating into our everyday actions and ongoing relationships God's new heaven and new earth revealed and brought near in Jesus Christ.

Because of the new heaven and new earth brought in Jesus Christ, we work for the healing of creation and for justice for all peoples.

We live without barriers because we know that God has reconciled all things and that all people are beloved children of God. We shun violence and vengeance for we know the peacemakers "will be called children of God" (Matthew 5:9) and "those who are persecuted for righteousness' sake" know that "theirs is the kingdom of heaven" (Matthew 5:10). We bring good news to the poor, release to captives, sight to the blind, and announce God's jubilee justice (Luke 4) because we know that the future belongs to Jesus' ministry. We protect the earth and its resources as a sign of our confidence in and commitment to God's healing of creation. We face death and sorrow knowing that "death has been swallowed up in victory" (1 Corinthians 15:54), that God "will wipe every tear from their eyes" and "death will be no more; mourning and crying and pain will be no more, for the first things have passed away" (Revelation 21:4). We "strive first for the kingdom of God and his righteousness" (Matthew 6:33), for we know that God's kingdom will come on earth as it is in heaven.

Since we believe that God will bring to completion what God began in Jesus Christ, we can live now with obedience born of hope and trust. Although evil, suffering, and death may continue to plague the earth, tempting us to disobedience and discouragement, we pursue Christlikeness with confidence and courage. We can look hatred and violence, injustice and exploitation, sin and death in the face and declare: You cannot win! Your doom is sure! In the words of Martin Luther:

> And though this world, with devils filled, should threaten to
>   undo us,
> we will not fear, for God hath willed his truth to triumph
>   through us.
> The Prince of Darkness grim, we tremble not for him;
> his rage we can endure, for lo, his doom is sure;
> one little word shall fell him.

> That word above all earthly powers, no thanks to them, abideth;
> the Spirit and the gifts are ours, through him who with us sideth.
> Let goods and kindred go, this mortal life also;
> the body they may kill; God's truth abideth still;
> his kingdom is forever.[9]

Conclusion

Much in the world seems to contradict belief in God's victory over death and sin. Sin continues to pervade every dimension of life, and death's reality intrudes into every person's encounters. Disease, poverty, and violence regularly destroy millions of God's children. Creation itself is threatened by climate change, pollution, exploitation, and abuse. As Chief, the homeless man, said, "The world ain't supposed to be like this."

The good news is this: One day, the world will not be like this! Another world—a world transformed by the eternal Word, made flesh in Jesus Christ—has come into being and triumphed. God's kingdom is coming! In Jesus Christ, a new world has dawned! God has begun a new heaven and a new earth. God will bring it to completion. We have been incorporated into Christ's death and resurrection. We faithfully and expectantly await the final victory. We are an Easter people who live now in the light of the coming dawn of God's eternal kingdom.

Several months after "Chief" was featured in the documentary on homelessness, his body was found floating down the Tennessee River. Apparently, he had fallen into the river and drowned. The church he visited weekly for lunch and attended occasionally for worship planned a memorial service for him. His family members from whom he had been alienated were contacted and the word was circulated among his friends who populated the homeless shelters and roamed the city streets. Notices of the memorial service were posted on the nearby University of Tennessee campus and among the professionals who worked in downtown offices.

The memorial service became a sign and foretaste of the new heaven and new earth. A large congregation of diverse people gathered to pay tribute and share grief—rich and poor, young and old, professional and the unskilled, professors and persons who could not read, the addicted and those in recovery, the insiders and the outsiders. Stories of experiences with Chief were told amid tears and laughter. Barriers crumbled, reconciliation appeared, hope surfaced, and commitment to care for one another emerged. At Chief's memorial service, for a brief time, the world was what it was supposed to be and what it is going to be!

John Wesley's last audible words before his death in 1791 affirm the faith that had shaped his life: "The best of all is, God is with us."[10] As heirs of Wesley, United Methodists live the belief that God has been with us, God is with us, and God shall be with us; and the whole creation will be transformed into God's New Heaven and New Earth! Living that belief is the United Methodist way.

Opportunities for Reflection/Discussion

The following questions may be used by groups wishing to discuss the material in chapter eleven or by individuals wanting to reflect on issues raised within the chapter.

1. What do you believe about the End or the Second Coming? How do your beliefs affect how you feel about the future and how you live today?

2. Do you agree that God's saving and reconciling action in Jesus Christ includes all creation? What are the implications of such a belief for such issues as the environment, medicine, scientific and technological development, poverty, or international conflict?

3. In what ways do beliefs in life after death and God's ultimate victory over sin and death bring hope and courage? In what ways do such beliefs bring judgment?

4. Have you read any of the *Left Behind* series? Why do you think the books have been so popular, having sold more than fifty million copies? What is your response to the critique of the series by Dr. Craig Hill in this chapter?

NOTES

Foreword

1. Sermon 122, "Causes of the Inefficacy of Christianity," *The Works of John Wesley* 54:86–96.

Introduction

1. See Nathan Hatch, *The Democratization of American Religion* (New Haven: Yale University Press, 1989).

2. From "Thoughts Upon Methodism," by John Wesley, in *The Works of John Wesley*, Vol. 9: The Methodist Societies: History, Nature, and Design, edited by Rupert E. Davies (Nashville, TN: Abingdon, 1989), 527.

Chapter 1

1. From *The Life Experience and Gospel of the Rt. Rev. Richard Allen*, by Richard Allen (Nashville, TN: Abingdon, 1983), 30.

2. Ibid.

3. From *The Book of Discipline of The United Methodist Church—2008*, 41.

4. Ibid., 44.

5. Ibid., 45.

6. Ibid.

7. Ibid.

8. From *The Life Experience and Gospel of the Rt. Rev. Richard Allen*, by Richard Allen (Nashville, TN: Abingdon, 1983), 29.

Chapter 2

1. From "Thoughts upon Methodism," by John Wesley, in *The Works of John Wesley*, Vol. 9: The Methodist Societies: History, Nature, and Design, edited by Rupert E. Davies (Nashville, TN: Abingdon, 1989), 527.

2. From *The Book of Discipline of The United Methodist Church—2008*, 50.

3. Ibid.

4. Ibid., 48.

5. From "On Living without God," (Sermon 130), by John Wesley, in *The Works of John Wesley*, Vol. 4: Sermons IV: 115-151, edited by Albert C. Outler (Nashville, TN: Abingdon, 1987), 175.

6. From *The Source*, by James Michener (Random House, 1965), 120.

7. As cited in *Context for Discovery*, by Neal F. Fisher (Nashville, TN: Abingdon, 1981), 17.

8. From *Mein Kampf*, by Adolf Hitler (Houghton Mifflin Company, 1943), 65. Emphasis original.

9. From "On Living Without God" (Sermon 130), by John Wesley, in *The Works of John Wesley*, Vol. 4: Sermons IV: 115-151, edited by Albert C. Outler (Nashville, TN: Abingdon, 1987), 171.

10. From *Existentialism*, by Jean-Paul Sartre, translated by B. Frechtman (Philosophical Library, 1947), 61.

11. See *God the Economist: The Doctrine of God and Political Economy*, by M. Douglas Meeks (Fortress, 1989).

12. See *Consuming Religion: Christian Faith and Practice in a Consumerist Culture*, by Vincent J. Miller (Continuum, 2005).

13. R. Laurence Moore, *Selling God* (New York: Oxford, 1994), 5.

14. From "The Use of Money," by John Wesley, in *The Works of John Wesley*. A five-session study of Wesley's approach to stewardship entitled, *Living for Giving: A Wesleyan View of Stewardship*, written by Kenneth L. Carder, is available from the United Methodist Foundation of Western North Carolina, Inc., P.O. Box 18005, Charlotte, NC 28218. The study includes written materials and a DVD.

15. From *Webster's New World Collegiate Dictionary*, third edition (Macmillan, 1996); s.v. hedonism, 625.

16. From "The Way of the Kingdom" (Sermon 7), by John Wesley, in *The Works of John Wesley*, Vol. 4: Sermons I:1-33, edited by Albert C. Outler (Nashville, TN: Abingdon, 1987), 223.

17. Ibid., 224.

18. From *Not Every Spirit: A Dogmatics of Christian Disbelief*, by Christopher Morse (Trinity Press International, 1994), 5.

19. From "The Way of the Kingdom" (Sermon 7), by John Wesley, in *The Works of John Wesley*, Vol. 4: Sermons I:1-33, edited by Albert C. Outler (Nashville, TN: Abingdon, 1987), 219.

20. Ibid., 220.

Chapter 3

1. From *Night*, by Elie Wiesel (Bantam Books, 1960), 62.

2. Alfred Tennyson, "In Memoria."

3. See Richard Dawkins, *The God Delusion*; Sam Harris, *The End of Faith*; and Christopher Hitchens, *God Is Not Great*.

4. From *The Book of Discipline of The United Methodist Church—2008*, 43.

5. Ibid.

6. From, "Hark! The Herald Angels Sing," by Charles Wesley, in *The United Methodist Hymnal* (Nashville, TN: The United Methodist Publishing House, 1989), 240. Used by permission.

7. From "A Service of Word and Table I," in *The United Methodist Hymnal* (Nashville, TN: The United Methodist Publishing House, 1989), 9. Used by permission.

8. From "A Modern Affirmation," in *The United Methodist Hymnal* (Nashville, TN: The United Methodist Publishing House, 1989), 885. Used by permission.

9. From *Not Every Spirit: A Dogmatics of Christian Disbelief*, by Christopher Morse (Trinity Press International, 1994), 180.

10. Ibid., 181.

11. "Holy Spirit, Come, Confirm Us," by Brian Foley (Copyright 1971 by Faber Music, Limited). Appears in *The United Methodist Hymnal*, 331.

12. From *The Book of Discipline of The United Methodist Church—2008*, 59.

13. From *Letters and Papers from Prison*, by Dietrich Bonhoeffer, edited by Eberhard Bethge (Macmillian Company, 1953), 361.

14. From *Process and Reality: An Essay in Cosmology*, by Alfred North Whitehead, corrected edition, edited by David Ray Griffin and Donald W. Sherburne (Free Press, 1978), 351.

15. From *Wesley and the People Called Methodists*, by Richard P. Heitzenrater (Nashville, TN: Abingdon, 1995), 308.

16. From "I'll Praise My Maker While I've Breath," by Isaac Watts in *The United Methodist Hymnal* (Nashville, TN: The United Methodist Publishing House, 1989), 60. Used by permission.

Chapter 4

1. From "The Divine Image" (Sermon 141), by John Wesley, in *The Works of John Wesley*, Vol. 4: Sermons IV, edited by Albert C. Outler (Nashville, TN: Abingdon, 1987), 290.

2. From "A Caution against Bigotry" (Sermon 38), by John Wesley, in *The Works of John Wesley*, Vol. 2: Sermons II: 34-70, edited by Albert C. Outler (Nashville, TN: Abingdon, 1985), 76.

3. From *Night*, by Elie Wiesel (Bantam Books, 1960), 62.

4. See Wesley's sermon, "General Deliverance of the Gospel" and his *A Survey of the Wisdom of God in Creation*, 4th ed. (London: Paramore, 1784), 4:22. Also see, Sermon 26, "Sermons on the Mount," III.7, in *The Works of John Wesley* (Nashville, TN: Abingdon, 1984), V. I, 581f.

5. This insight comes primarily from M. Douglas Meeks in his book *God the Economist: The Doctrine of God and Political Economy* (Fortress, 1989).

6. See "The Image of God" (Sermon 141), by John Wesley, in *The Works of John Wesley*, Vol. 4: Sermons IV; 115-151, edited by Albert C. Outler (Nashville, TN: Abingdon, 1987), 292ff. Also, see "Toward a Wesleyan Social Ethic," by James C. Logan, in *Wesleyan Theology Today: A Bicentennial Theological Consultation*, edited by Theodore Runyon (Kingswood Books, 1985), 365.

7. From "Salvation by Faith" (Sermon 1), by John Wesley, in *The Works of John Wesley*, Vol. 1: Sermons I:1-33, edited by Albert C. Outler (Nashville, TN: Abingdon, 1984), 117.

8. From *Not Every Spirit: A Dogmatics of Christian Disbelief*, by Christopher Morse (Trinity Press International, 1994), 265.

9. From "Sermon on the Mount XIII," (Sermon 33) by John Wesley, in *The Works of John Wesley*, vol.2, edited by Albert C. Outler (Nashville, TN: Abingdon, 1985).

Chapter 5

1. From *The Book of Discipline of The United Methodist Church—2008*, 61.

2. Ibid., 68.

3. See "The Image of God" (Sermon 141), by John Wesley, in *The Works of John Wesley*, Vol. 4: Sermons IV: 115-151, edited by Albert C. Outler (Nashville, TN: Abingdon, 1987), 292ff.

4. From "The One Thing Needful" (Sermon 146), by John Wesley, in *The Works of John Wesley*, Vol. 4: Sermons IV: 115-151, edited by Albert C. Outler (Nashville, TN: Abingdon, 1987), 354.

5. Ibid.

6. From *The Book of Discipline of The United Methodist Church—2008*, 61.

7. Ibid.

8. From "Original Sin" (Sermon 44), by John Wesley, in *The Works of John Wesley*, Vol. 2: Sermons II: 34-70, edited by Albert C. Outler (Nashville, TN: Abingdon, 1985), 172.

9. From "Original Sin" (Sermon 44), by John Wesley, in *The Works of John Wesley*, Vol. 2: Sermons II: 34-70, edited by Albert C. Outler (Nashville, TN: Abingdon, 1985), 173.

10. See *Whatever Became of Sin?* by Karl Menninger (Hawthorne Books, 1973).

11. *The New York Times*, January 8, 1992.

12. From "Depth of Mercy," by Charles Wesley, in *The United Methodist Hymnal* (Nashville, TN: The United Methodist Publishing House, 1989), 357. Used by permission.

13. From "Original Sin" (Sermon 44), by John Wesley, in *The Works of John Wesley*, Vol. 2: Sermons II:34-70, edited by Albert C. Outler (Nashville, TN: Abingdon, 1985), 185.

Chapter 6

1. From *The Book of Discipline of The United Methodist Church*, 43.

2. From "The End of Christ's Coming" (Sermon 62), by John Wesley, in *The Works of John Wesley*, Vol. 2: Sermons II:34-70, edited by Albert C. Outler (Nashville, TN: Abingdon, 1985), 482-483.

3. "Introduction," by Albert C. Outler, in *The Works of John Wesley*, Vol. 1: Sermons I:1-33, edited by Albert C. Outler (Nashville, TN: Abingdon, 1984), 13.

4. From *The Book of Discipline of The United Methodist Church—2008*, 45.

5. Ibid.

6. Ibid.

7. Ibid., 46.

8. From "Salvation by Faith" (Sermon 1), by John Wesley, in *The Works of John Wesley*, Vol. 1: Sermons 1-33, edited by Albert C. Outler (Nashville, TN: Abingdon, 1984), 117-118.

9. See Randy Maddox, *Responsible Grace*.

10. From "Letter to Alexander Knox," October 26, 1778, *Letters* (Telford edition), Vol. 6, 327.

11. From *The Book of Discipline of The United Methodist Church—2008*, 46.

12. From "A Plain Account of the People Called Methodists, in a Letter to the Rev. Mr. Perronet, Vicar of Shoreham in Kent," by John Wesley, in *The Works of John Wesley*, Vol 9: The Methodist Societies: History, Nature, and Design, edited by Rupert E. Davies (Nashville, TN: Abingdon, 1989), 256-257.

13. From "The Scripture Way of Salvation," (Sermon 43), in *The Works of John Wesley*, Vol. 1: Sermons II: 34-70, edited by Albert C. Outler (Nashville, TN: Abingdon, 1985), 157.

14. From *The Book of Discipline of The United Methodist Church—2008*, 46.

15. From "Journal: From February 1, 1737/38 to September 16, 1738," by John Wesley, in *The Works of John Wesley*, Vol 18: Journal and Diaries I (1735-1738), edited by W. Reginald Ward and Richard P. Heitzenrater (Nashville, TN: Abingdon, 1988), 249-250.

16. From *The Book of Discipline of The United Methodist Church—2008*, 46.

17. Ibid., 47.

18. From "On Perfection" (Sermon 76), by John Wesley, in *The Works of John Wesley*, Vol. 3: Sermons III:71-114, edited by Albert C. Outler (Nashville, TN: Abingdon, 1986), 74.

19. See *A Plain Account of Christian Perfection*, John Wesley (London: The Epworth Press, reprinted 1973), 52.

20. From "Love Divine, All Loves Excelling," by Charles Wesley, in *The United Methodist Hymnal* (Nashville, TN: The United Methodist Publishing House, 1989), 384. Used by permission.

21. See Jackson edition, *Wesley Works*, Vol. 14 (Grand Rapids: Baker Book House, 1979), 321.

22. From "What is Methodism's Theological Contribution Today?", by Theodore Runyon, in *Wesleyan Theology Today: A Bicentennial Theological Consultation*, edited by Theodore Runyon (Kingswood Books, 1985), 12.

Chapter 7

1. This is a phrase Wesley used to describe the Christian life and his primary desire.

2. From *The Book of Discipline of The United Methodist Church—2008*, 47.

3. Ibid., 48.

4. Some Moravians held this position.

5. From *The Book of Discipline of The United Methodist Church—2008*, 73.

6. From "Journal: From February 1, 1737/38 to September 16, 1738," by John Wesley, in *The Works of John Wesley*, Vol. 18: Journals and Diaries I (1735-1738), edited by W. Reginald Ward and Richard P. Heitzenrater (Nashville, TN: Abingdon, 1988), 228.

7. From *The Book of Discipline of The United Methodist Church—2008*, 73-74.

8. From *Three Simple Rules: A Wesleyan Way of Living*, by Rueben P. Job. (Nashville, TN: Abingdon, 2007), 7.

9. Ibid., 51ff.

10. From *The Book of Discipline of The United Methodist Church—2008*, 72.

11. From *Wesley and the People Called Methodists*, by Richard P. Heitzenrater (Nashville, TN: Abingdon, 1995), 199.

12. From "Rules of the Band Societies, Drawn up December 25, 1738," by John Wesley, in *The Works of John Wesley*, Vol. 9: The Methodist Societies: History, Nature, and Design, edited by Rupert E. Davies (Nashville, TN: Abingdon, 1989), 199.

13. From *The Cost of Discipleship*, by Dietrich Bonhoeffer (Macmillian Company, 1959), 45, 47.

14. From "Jesus United by Thy Love," by Charles Wesley, in *The United Methodist Hymnal* (Nashville, TN: The United Methodist Publishing House, 1989), 561. Used by permission.

15. From "A Covenant Prayer in the Wesleyan Tradition," in *The United Methodist Hymnal* (Nashville, TN: The United Methodist Publishing House, 1989), 607. Used by permission. This is a twentieth-century adaptation of

the prayer Wesley and the early Methodists used. This modern version may misconstrue the sense of costly discipleship by changing "exalted for thee, or trodden under foot for thee" to "brought low by thee."

Chapter 8

1. See *Three Simple Rules,* by Rueben P. Job (Nashville, TN: Abingdon, 2008), 53ff.

2. From *The Book of Discipline of The United Methodist Church—2008,* 74.

3. From "Minutes of Some Late Conversations between The Rev. Mr. Wesley and Others," in *Wesley's Works,* Vol. 8: "Addresses, Essays, Letters," (Reprinted 1979 by Baker Book House Company from 1872 edition), 322.

4. From *The Book of Discipline of The United Methodist Church—2008,* 70.

5. From "Love Divine, All Loves Excelling," by Charles Wesley, in *The United Methodist Hymnal* (Nashville, TN: The United Methodist Publishing House, 1989), 384. Used by permission.

6. See "The Basic Pattern of Worship," in *The United Methodist Book of Worship,* (Nashville, TN: The United Methodist Publishing House, 1992), 13ff.

7. From "The Confession of Faith of the Evangelical United Brethren Church, Article VI—The Sacraments," in *The Book of Discipline of The United Methodist Church—2008,* 68.

8. Ibid.

9. Ibid.

10. From "Sermon on the Mount—Discourse Six," by John Wesley; quoted in *This Holy Mystery: A United Methodist Understanding of Holy Communion,* adopted by the 2004 General Conference of The United Methodist Church (Copyright 2003, 2004, The General Board of Discipleship of The United Methodist Church), 5.

11. From *The Book of Discipline of The United Methodist Church—2008,* 68.

12. From "A Service of Word and Table I," in *The United Methodist Hymnal* (Nashville, TN: The United Methodist Publishing House, 1989), 11. Used by permission.

13. From "A Service of Word and Table I," in *The United Methodist Hymnal* (Nashville, TN: The United Methodist Publishing House, 1989), 7. Used by permission.

14. *This Holy Mystery* is an excellent resource for understanding Holy Communion and it provides strong rationale for weekly celebration.

15. From *Three Simple Rules: A Wesleyan Way of Living,* by Rueben P. Job (Nashville, TN: Abingdon, 2008), 54.

16. From "The Means of Grace," (Sermon 16), by John Wesley, in *The Works of John Wesley,* Vol. 1: Sermons I:1-33, edited by Albert C. Outler (Nashville, TN: Abingdon, 1984), 384.

17. From *The Book of Discipline of The United Methodist Church—2008,* 67.

18. From "The Preface to Sermons on Several Occasions," by John Wesley, in *The Works of John Wesley*, Vol. 1: Sermons I:1-33, edited by Albert C. Outler (Nashville, TN: Abingdon, 1984), 105.

19. From "A Short History of the People Called Methodists," by John Wesley, in *The Works of John Wesley*, Vol. 9: The Methodist Societies: History, Nature, and Design, edited by Rupert E. Davies (Nashville, TN: Abingdon, 1989), 484.

20. From *Soul Feast: An Invitation to the Christian Spiritual Life*, by Marjorie Thompson (Westminster John Knox Press, 2005), 71.

21. From "Minutes of Some Late Conversations between The Rev. Mr. Wesley and Others," in *Wesley's Works*, Vol. 8: "Addresses, Essays, Letters," (Reprinted 1979 by Baker Book House Company from 1872 edition), 323.

Chapter 9

1. From "Of the Church" (Sermon 74), by John Wesley, in *The Works of John Wesley*, Vol. 3: Sermons III: 71-114, edited by Albert C. Outler (Nashville, TN: Abingdon, 1986), 46.

2. From *Biblical Perspectives on Evangelism*, by Walter Brueggemann (Nashville, TN: Abingdon, 1993), 90f.

3. From *The Book of Discipline of The United Methodist Church—2008*, 45.

4. Ibid., 67-68.

5. Ibid., 87.

6. Ibid.

7. For a helpful discussion of the basic qualities of the church's mission see Robert Schanase's *Five Practices of Fruitful Congregations*, (Nashville, TN: Abingdon, 2007). The five practices listed are "Radical Hospitality," "Passionate Worship," "Intentional Faith Development," "Risk-taking Mission and Service," and "Extravagant Generosity."

8. From "On God's Vineyard" (Sermon 107), by John Wesley, in *The Works of John Wesley*, Vol. 3: Sermons III:71-114, edited by Albert C. Outler (Nashville, TN: Abingdon, 1986), 510.

9. From "Catholic Spirit" (Sermon 39), by John Wesley, in *The Works of John Wesley*, Vol. 2: Sermons II: 34-70, edited by Albert C. Outler (Nashville, TN: Abingdon, 1985), 93.

10. See Donald E. Messer and William J. Abraham, editors, *Unity, Liberty, and Charity: Building Bridges under Icy Waters* (Nashville, TN: Abingdon, 1996).

11. From "Catholic Spirit" (Sermon 39), by John Wesley, in *The Works of John Wesley*, Vol. 2: Sermons II: 34-70, edited by Albert C. Outler (Nashville, TN: Abingdon, 1985), 93.

Chapter 10

1. From *The Book of Discipline of The United Methodist Church—2008*, 75.

2. From "Conciliar Theology: A Report" by Thomas A. Langford, in *Quarterly Review*; Summer 1989, 9.

3. Ibid.

4. For a comprehensive and accessible treatment of the "Quadrilateral" see *Wesley and the Quadrilateral*, edited by Stephen Gunter, (Nashville, TN: Abingdon, 1997).

5. From *The Book of Discipline of The United Methodist Church—2008*, 60.

6. From *A Plain Account of Christian Perfection*, by John Wesley (Epworth Press, 1952), 6.

7. From "Introduction," by Albert C. Outler, in *The Works of John Wesley*, Vol. 1: Sermons I: 1-33, edited by Albert C. Outler (Nashville, TN: Abingdon, 1984), 57.

8. For a comprehensive treatment of Wesley's use of scripture, see Scott J. Jones, *John Wesley's Conception and Use of Scripture* (Nashville, TN: Kingswood Books, 1995).

9. *Disciple Bible Study* is a systematic and creative resource for in-depth study of the Bible produced and published by The United Methodist Publishing House and available through Cokesbury.

10. From *The Book of Discipline of The United Methodist Church—2008*, 79.

11. From "Address to the Clergy," by John Wesley, *The Works of John Wesley* (Jackson edition), Vol. 10, 484.

12. From *The Book of Discipline of The United Methodist Church—2008*, 81.

13. Ibid., 82.

14. From "A Letter to the Rev. Dr. Rutherford," by John Wesley, in *The Letters of the Rev. John Wesley, A.M.*, standard edition, edited by John Telford (Epworth Press, 1931), 364.

15. From *The Book of Discipline of The United Methodist Church—2008*, 83.

16. See Theodore W. Jennings' *Loyalty to God: The Apostles' Creed in Life and Liturgy* (Nashville, TN: Abingdon, 1992).

Chapter 11

1. From "The General Spread of the Gospel" (Sermon 63), by John Wesley, in *The Works of John Wesley*, Vol. 2: Sermons II: 34-70, edited by Albert C. Outler (Nashville, TN: Abingdon, 1985), 485.

2. Ibid., 488.

3. From *The Book of Discipline of The United Methodist Church—2008*, 44.

4. From *The United Methodist Hymnal* (Nashville, TN: The United Methodist Publishing House, 1989), 10. Used by permission.

5. From *The United Methodist Hymnal* (Nashville, TN: The United Methodist Publishing House, 1989), 880, 881, and 884. Used by permission.

6. From *In God's Time: The Bible and The Future*, by Craig C. Hill (William B. Eerdmans Publishing Company, 2002), 207.

7. From "The General Spread of the Gospel" (Sermon 63), by John Wesley, in *The Works of John Wesley*, Vol. 2: Sermons II: 34-70, edited by Albert C. Outler (Nashville, TN: Abingdon, 1985), 499.

8. From "The New Creation" (Sermon 64), by John Wesley, in *The Works of John Wesley*, Vol. 2: Sermons II: 34-70, edited by Albert C. Outler (Nashville, TN: Abingdon, 1985), 509.

9. From "A Mighty Fortress Is Our God," by Martin Luther, in *The United Methodist Hymnal* (Nashville, TN: The United Methodist Publishing House, 1989), 110. Used by permission.

10. From *Wesley and the People Called Methodists*, by Richard P. Heitzenrater (Nashville, TN: Abingdon, 1985), 308.